How It All Began
in the
Pantry

Author's Note

Bringing together a book such as this takes a tremendous amount of time, quite as much in the research as in the writing, but it has been a fascinating and rewarding opportunity and has certainly provided me with much food for thought! The work has involved a great deal of searching in magazines, journals and old books on food, as well as contacting many of the companies whose brand names we most associate with the foods we eat today. I have also made many visits to towns and villages where some of our foods originated, as well as visiting or corresponding with their local libraries.

Throughout I have found staff who have been most helpful, archivists who have been only too willing to provide historical information and illustrative material, and companies and individuals who have kindly given me their time and passed on their knowledge. To everyone concerned, I really do appreciate your co-operation.

The selection of foodstuffs available to us today is simply too vast for me to have included a history of them all within the confines of this book. I have therefore tried to concentrate on firm favourites in most cases, with a dash of more obscure or forgotten foods in others. As I sought for information on the history of food, I have been surprised by how little documented material exists in some areas. However, this has only been an incentive to search out the answers. This I have done to the best of my ability, and readers may be interested to know that many of the stories, pictures and advertisements in this book have not been published for over a hundred years.

I would especially like to thank the following for their special help: Tom and Peggy Hewitt, Lady Mountbatten, Susanna Geoghegan, Dr Fred Kidd, Business Archives Council, The Sea Fish Industry Authority, Baxters, Eden Vale, Liverpool Central Library, Lyons Cakes, Robertson's, Quiggin's, Warburtons, Wilkin & Sons Ltd, Whitstable Museum and Gallery, Chelsea Library and the staff at Michael O'Mara Books, especially Jacquie Wines, my editor, Judith Palmer and Suzanne Paterson. If I have omitted anyone, I apologize; it is not intentional, but the text has been gathered from a vast number of sources.

Finally, I want to acknowledge the vast amount of reading and research my wife Judith has done on my behalf; without her support this book could not have been brought to fruition. It is therefore with my love and sincere thanks that I dedicate it to her.

Bibliography

The following is not so much a list of books to which I have referred, but a guide to where interested readers may find further information on the history of food should they wish:

Magazines: *Chambers's Journals*, 1890–1910 issues; *Household Guide*, 1870; *The Graphic* (various issues); *The Illustrated London News* (various issues), *Punch* (various issues).

Books: *A Gourmet's Guide*, John Ayto, Oxford University Press, 1994; *A Hundred Wonderful Years*, Mrs C. S. Peel, Bodley Head, 1926; *Folklore & Odysseys of Food and Medicinal Plants*, E. & J. Lehner, Harrap, 1973; *Food and Drink in Britain*, C. Anne Wilson, Penguin Books, 1973; *Larousse Gastronomique*, P. Montagne, Hamlyn, 1961; *Mrs Beeton's Book of Household Management* (1909 edition), Ward Lock; *Spons' Household Manual: A Treasury of Domestic Receipts*, E. & F. N. Spon, 1891; *The Modern Baker*, John Kirkland, Gresham, 1924; *The Modern Grocer*, edited by W. G. Copsey, Caxton, 1951; *The London Ritz Book of Afternoon Tea: The Art & Pleasures of Taking Tea*, Helen Simpson, Ebury Press, 1986; *Time for Tea, A Book of Days*, compiled by Jane Pettigrew, Little, Brown and Company (UK) Ltd, 1991.

There is also an increasing number of informative websites on the Internet.

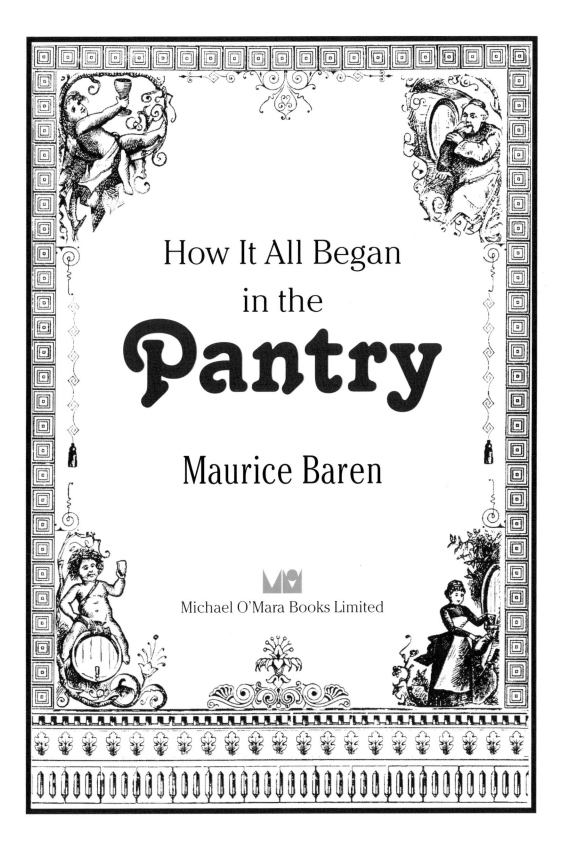

How It All Began
in the
Pantry

Maurice Baren

Michael O'Mara Books Limited

Maurice Baren was born in Harrogate, Yorkshire. After a long career in horticulture and landscape management, he has now dedicated himself to discovering many aspects of our social history and bringing them to the notice of an increasing number of readers. His earlier titles are *How It All Began*, his first book about the history behind certain brand names, *How It All Began in the Garden*, *How It All Began Up the High Street*, *How Household Names Began*, *How It All Began in Yorkshire*, *Victorian Shopping*, and *How It All Began in Lancashire*.

First published in Great Britain in 2000 by
Michael O'Mara Books Limited
9 Lion Yard, Tremadoc Road
London SW4 7NQ

A CIP catalogue record for this book is available from the British Library

ISBN 1-85479-448-5

3 5 7 9 10 8 6 4 2

Designed and typeset by Martin Bristow

Printed and bound in Italy by L.E.G.O., Vicenza

Contents

Preface

The very word 'pantry' conjures up images of shelves full of home-made produce filled with wholesome ingredients. Lurking behind those commodities that may seem commonplace to us – tomato ketchup, marmalade, cocoa, Liquorice Allsorts, even tins of Spam – are stories and people that will make even a simple sausage seem special. After all, everything we eat was in the first instance somebody's bright idea.

Certainly we British enjoy our food and never before have we had such a range and variety of foodstuffs available to us. However, the origins of our food have in many cases been overlooked or forgotten. Who were John Dory, Granny Smith and the mysterious ladies behind two popular puddings – Apple Charlotte and Crêpes Suzette? The 'Reine Claude'

was a sixteenth-century French fruit now widely eaten in Britain under another name. What? And why?

It is a wise man who spots a gap in the market and an enterprising one who successfully fills it. In 1908 a Manchester herbalist launched a fruit cordial that he claimed would fill the nation with 'vim and vigour'. There was a bill going through Parliament at the time to restrict opening hours at public houses. People would be thirsty. Hence Vimto was born.

What had Napoleon to do with advances in the preserving of food? Is there a connection between Nell Gwynne and Express Dairies? What kind of soup was 'pittance'? Baked Alaska was a cosmopolitan dish that actually originated in China. Why?

The full stories behind these fascinating tit-bits about the history of our food and many more culinary insights are to be found in *How It All Began in the Pantry*. In 300 BC the Greek philosopher Epicurus wrote: 'Eating is one of life's great pleasures.' He was right!

Naughty But Nice!
CAKES & BISCUITS

Most of us enjoy a nice bun, cake or biscuit – even if they are bad for our figures! Our fondness for a sweet treat has meant that, over the years, many regions, towns, individual people and, indeed, days of the year have become renowned for a particular delicacy.

Bath seems to have more such favourites than most places, among them the Sally Lunn bun, the Bath bun and the Bath Oliver biscuit. Sally Lunn, originally Soli (Solange) Luyon, was a Huguenot girl who fled from France in 1680 and found work with a baker who had premises in Lilliput Alley, now North Parade Passage, not far from Bath Abbey. The building where she worked still stands and is now the oldest house in Bath, dating back to 1482. It was while the building was being renovated in the 1930s that the original recipe for Sally Lunns was found in a secret cupboard over the downstairs corner fireplace. The recipe for these large, round, teacake-like buns, which is still a secret, passes with the deeds of the property from one owner to the next.

In the cuisine of France there are eight basic doughs. However many there were in Bath in Sally's day, *brioche* was not known at the bakers where she was employed. So Sally introduced customers to a new brioche-type bun and it was a great success, the bun taking her name. Sally Lunns were served at public breakfasts and at the afternoon teas that were to become as much a part of Bath's tradition as the taking of the waters at the spa; tea at the Pump Room in Bath is still a favourite with visitors to the city today.

Sally Lunn and her famous house at Bath.

The buns are made in special Sally Lunn or muffin rings, about 4 inches in diameter. The original oven in which the Sally Lunns were baked was made of stone and burnt faggots – tightly-tied bundles of thin branches. When these had been set alight, air was drawn in at the bottom of the oven and smoke escaped through a vent at the top. The hot embers were then raked out and the floor of the oven was swept clean with a scuffle – a wet sackcloth swinging on the end of a pole – and the dough was baked on the heat stored in the stone. In Georgian times they were served with curd cheese and cured ham; today they are usually cut in half horizontally, toasted on both the cut surfaces, spread with softened butter, and topped with strawberry jam and cream. Delicious!

Hot, buttered Sally Lunns were advertised in verse in the *Bath Chronicle* in the mid-1700s and even found their way into Gilbert and Sullivan's operetta *The Sorcerer* in the words of the chorus: 'Now for the muffins and toast and now for the gay Sally Lunn'. Charles Dickens also wrote about 'Sally Lunn, the illustrious author of a tea cake'.

The Bath Oliver is an unsweetened biscuit named after Dr William Oliver (1695–1764) who invented them. He was a physician at the Bath Mineral Water Hospital and he intended his biscuit to be an aid to healthy digestion and weight loss. By the nineteenth century the biscuits had become very popular. Today they are made by Jacobs and are stocked by most supermarkets, and William Oliver's picture is on every biscuit.

The cake that is most commonly associated with this city, of course, is the Bath bun, or the Bath cake as it was sometimes called. Bath buns are traditionally made from a plain dough without any dried fruit being added, although they were once topped with tiny sweets

good cheese *is better with*

FORTT'S
BATH OLIVER
Biscuits

being rather square in shape. The buns were created by the Hands family, who were bakers, and were sold from the Old Chelsea Bun House on Grosvenor Row, now part of Pimlico Road in Westminster. Chelsea buns must date from at least the early eighteenth century for they are mentioned, somewhat unflatteringly, in Jonathan Swift's *Journal to Stella* (2 May 1711): 'Was it not *Rrrrrrrrare* Chelsea buns [a street vendor's cry]? I bought one to-day in my walk; it cost me a penny; it was stale, and I did not like it.'

Whatever Swift may have thought of that particular bun, Chelsea buns were hugely popular. Records show that 240,000 buns were sold on Good Friday alone in 1829. However, as the

containing caraway seeds, or had sugar lumps concealed inside them, a pleasurable discovery for those with a sweet tooth! Records show that William Fortt of Bath was making the buns in the late 1830s and *The Experienced English Housekeeper*, an eighteenth-century cookbook, gives the following recipe for Bath cakes:

> Rub half a pound of butter into a pound of flour and one spoonful of good barm. Warm some cream and make it into a light paste, set it on the fire to rise. When you make them up, take four ounces of caraway comfits, work part of them in, and strew the rest on the top, make them into a round cake, the size of a French roll, bake them on sheet tins and send them in hot for breakfast.

Today's Bath buns are generally sold round and flattish and are about 3 to 4 inches across. Most will have a sprinkling of currants and sugar added to the top of the bun.

Similar to the Bath bun is the Chelsea bun, a rolled yeast bun, dense with currants, sugar, lemon rind and spice and decorated with sugar, although this bun has the distinction of

Chelsea Bun House was also famous for its hot-cross buns, it is more likely that this figure was for hot-cross buns. For reasons unknown, the Chelsea Bun House was pulled down in 1839. Sadly, we don't have the original recipe, but Chelsea buns are still sold in most bakers and supermarkets. Fitzbillies, a bakery established by the Mason brothers in Cambridge in the early 1920s, claims to be renowned for its Chelsea buns, sending them all round the world. They keep their recipe a closely-guarded secret and say of their bun: 'The original Fitzbillies Chelsea Bun is probably the stickiest in the world and has been our most popular product for over 75 years. It is rich, spicy, syrupy and travels extremely well.'

Another long-time favourite, dating from the eighteenth century, is the Banbury cake. *People's Magazine* of 1867 tells us how passengers travelling to London on the south-west train were greeted with cries of 'Banbury Cakes! Real Banbury Cakes!' when the train pulled into Banbury station. Neat little packages of this delightful comestible were passed to weary travellers through the carriage windows, before once again the train pulled

away to complete its journey. Banbury cakes certainly made an impression on the writer of this piece, for he also recalls eating them some fifty years earlier:

> they were – as crisp, as tender, as seductive, as well qualified to enhance one's anticipations at every bite, without cloying one with complete and entire satisfaction – which prudent and delicate reserve on their part constitutes indeed their perfection …
> the mysterious combination of an outward fact of frosted sugar with an inner idea of pastry and mincemeat.

Betty White, the proprietress of the Original Cake Shop, situated at 12 Parsons Street, Banbury, was the creator of the Banbury cake. Old Jarvis White, Betty's husband, is said to have spent much of his day hanging over the hatch of the shop door while she worked inside, but he was proud of his wife's cakes and liked to tell customers how 'a sparrow came into the shop one day and flew off with one'. The pastry from which the Banbury cakes are made is a mix of flour, fat, water and salt. The filling is made of currants, peel, flour, butter, brown sugar, rose water, lemon essence, rum essence and nutmeg. The cake starts out as a small ball containing the filling and is then rolled by hand into a cigar-shape, before being flattened, marked with a criss-cross pattern and given a dusting of a mix of caster and icing sugar.

In 1841 there was a substantial trade with India for Banbury cakes, a trade which continued for many years – the cakes arriving there safely, packed in airtight tins and well preserved from hungry sailors. The cakes are still made to the original recipe by master

ABOVE: *The Chelsea Bun House.*
RIGHT: *The Rutland Arms Hotel, the birthplace of the Bakewell pudding.*
BELOW RIGHT: *A true Bakewell pudding.*

bakers and those visiting Banbury should certainly find an excuse to be there at teatime.

The town of Eccles in Lancashire gives its name to the Eccles cake, which began to appear in the town's bakeries in 1796. James Birch, a corn miller and baker, started making the cakes at a shop opposite Eccles Parish Church in St Mary's Street – later renamed Church Street. However, in 1810 Birch moved his business to larger premises on the other side of the street. Keen not to lose business, he placed an advertisement outside his new shop stating 'Removed from across the way'. His original shop was now in the hands of one William Bradburn who had learnt cake making from Birch. Also keen to guard his interests, Bradburn chose to display his own sign, which declared 'Never Removed'. From then on Bradburn made the most of the fact that his were the premises where the now highly sought after Eccles cakes were first made.

By 1818 vast quantities of the small, round cakes, with their buttery, flaky pastry and currant filling, were not only sold throughout Britain but were exported to America and the West Indies. In 1879 Bradburn's claimed that they could make nine thousand cakes a day. James Birch's shop sadly closed and Bradburn's became the only shop in the town specializing in the making of Eccles cakes.

Although the original shop no longer stands, its nineteenth-century window frame is preserved in Peel Park Museum, Salford.

Eliza Acton's *Modern Cookery* of 1845 gives the following recipe for Bakewell pudding – not to be confused with the Bakewell tart, which is a modern corruption of the more traditional 'pudding'.

Line a shallow tart-dish with quite an inch deep layer of several kinds of good preserve mixed together, and intermingle with them from two to three ounzes [sic] of candied citron or orange-rind.

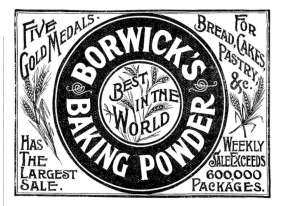

Beat well the yolks of ten eggs, and add to them gradually half a pound of sifted sugar; when they are well mixed, pour in by degrees half a pound of good clarified butter, and a little ratafia or any other flavour that may be preferred; fill the dish two thirds full with this mixture, and bake the pudding for nearly an hour in a moderate oven. Half the quantity will be sufficient for a small dish.

Eliza describes the pudding as rich and expensive but not as a very refined dish, preferring instead an Alderman's pudding, which omits the peel but has a layer of apricot jam.

However, others believe that the true Bakewell pudding began life at a later date. On the site of the old White Horse Inn, but newly built in 1804, stands the Rutland Arms Hotel in Bakewell. Legend has it that in the 1860s, a cook, employed by Mrs Greaves who kept the hotel, made the first Bakewell pudding – by accident. One day the cook mistakenly put jam in the bottom of the pudding case and the filling on top of it. When cooked, the pudding had an unusual dark top, but the guests complimented Mrs Greaves and she instructed the cook that, henceforth, the pudding should always be made in that way. Its ingredients are eggs, butter, jam, flaky pastry and a spot of almond essence – although as for the actual mixture, well that's a secret! The original 'pudding' fireplace and oven still exist within the hotel, although various bakeries in the town claim to have the 'secret recipe'.

Me for Mc Dougall's SELF-RAISING flour

– still the surest!

There have been many happy accidents when it comes to the creation of famous dishes, which should reassure anyone who is less than confident in the kitchen. *Tarte Tatin*, with its deeply caramelized apples and crispy pastry, is legendary throughout France. When Jean Tatin, proprietor of the Hôtel Tatin in Lamotte-Beuvron (a small rural town in the Loire Valley) died, his two daughters, Caroline and Stéphanie, took over the management of the hotel. The elder sister, Stéphanie, ran the kitchen and was a particularly fine cook. Her speciality was apple tart, but one lunchtime, during the busy hunting season, Stéphanie put her tart in the oven upside-down. She nevertheless served the dish, piping hot and straight from the oven, and received so many compliments that she made it that way from that day on. Today many chefs have added a variation or two to the tart – but it is always served upside-down and piping hot.

Other successes 'in the kitchen' have, in contrast, been carefully contrived. Let us pause a moment on Mr Kipling, whose cakes are baked by Manor Bakeries, now part of the Rank Hovis McDougall Group. Mr Kipling is probably the best-known name in commercial cake-making since 'his' cakes entered our shops in 1967. At that time there were very few small cakes in our supermarkets, and such as there were fared badly due to poor packaging. The leading cake makers of the time were seen as specialists in other fields – Lyons were the market leaders with their Corner Houses and tea, whilst Cadbury's and McVities were famous for chocolate and biscuits. There were no true cake brands and Manor Bakeries saw a gap in the market.

Their aim was to make large quantities of small cakes usually found in the local baker's shop, yet also to maintain quality, and to avoid the stigma of mass production. It was decided that the cakes should be thought of as being made by a person with a small bakery, someone who took infinite care with cakes – a true cake specialist. The cakes should be small and perfect, the sort that would be difficult to replicate at home, but that should also disguise any hint of commercial production. Thus Mr Kipling was born: middle-aged, kindly, traditional and making 'Exceedingly Good Cakes'. Within six months of achieving national

BELOW: *Lyons' Corner House in London's Piccadilly.*

LEFT: *Like Keiller, Goodfellow's have been baking Dundee cakes in Dundee for over 100 years.*

distribution Mr Kipling was a market leader. Today the company sells a range of forty products and has a turnover in the region of two hundred million pounds.

Another popular figure in the commercial cake world is Sara Lee who has cornered a large chunk of the market in frozen desserts. However, unlike Mr Kipling, Sara Lee does exist. She is the daughter of an American cheesecake maker, Charlie Lubin, who started out in business with his brother-in-law in 1935 with a small chain of shops called Community Bake Shops. In 1949, when Sara was eight years old, her father decided to move on independently and renamed his company after her. The company's move into frozen cakes developed due to the demand for their products further afield. In 1953 Sara Lee developed their own special process for freezing baked goods and also introduced foil containers, which were suitable to bake the product in later. These innovations made them market leaders in the United States. The company opened their first factory in Britain in 1977 at Bridlington, East Yorkshire. In 1984 they distributed goods to seventy different countries and the company continues to be hugely successful.

In Dundee, Keiller have been manufacturing marmalade for almost two hundred years, but it is with their Dundee cake that the town's name has become synonymous. Keiller began adding the left-over ingredients of their marmalade to a standard fruitcake recipe and thus created a cake unlike any other – rich with crystallized orange peel, sultanas and the zest of Seville oranges, and characterized by a topping of whole almonds. Once the cake had been baked, but while still warm, it was washed over with orange-juice syrup, which gave it an attractive glaze. The cake soon became a success both in Scotland and throughout the rest of the country. It is still a year-round teatime favourite with many people, but is also associated with Christmas tea, where it provides a lighter alternative to the traditional Christmas cake.

There are, of course, many seasonal cakes. The French have a Twelfth Night cake – the forerunner to our Christmas cake, and the Germans an Easter Torte. Simnel cake, a fruit cake with a layer of almond paste or marzipan baked in the centre, and sometimes coloured with saffron, is especially associated with Easter and mid-Lent. On the fourth Sunday in

Lent, Mothering Sunday, young girls who were in service were allowed to go home to visit their mothers and would take with them a Simnel cake. The fourth Sunday in Lent is also known as Refreshment Sunday, when the Gospel reading is on the Feeding of the Five Thousand, and on that day some relaxation was allowed from Lenten fasting. At Easter, Simnel cake is decorated with eleven small marzipan balls, which are supposed to represent the apostles. There are only eleven of them, however, because Judas betrayed Christ and is therefore not included. It is thought that the word 'Simnel' may derive from the Roman period when there was a type of bread called *simnellus*. The Greek word *semidalis* means fine flour, as does the Latin word *simila* and the Old French word *simenel*. However, the Anglo-Saxons had a word *symel* meaning a feast, so perhaps it derives from that.

Another festive fare is the mince pie. These were originally called 'minced pies'. In Sheppard's *Epigrams*, dated 1651, they are referred to as 'shrid-pies', 'shrid' meaning shredded and referring to the pies' filling. In a 1783 edition of *Gentleman's Magazine*, the writer suggests that the pies are symbolic of the offerings made by the Three Wise Men. A similar idea was in evidence in Victorian times, when the pies were often oval in shape, rather than round, to represent Jesus's crib. The original mincemeat filling contained meat, but as meat was expensive it was bulked out with sultanas. Interestingly, early advertisements for Robertson's mincemeat stated clearly that their produce was not to be confused with finely-chopped meat, thus avoiding any confusion of meat and sweetmeat. Today the only 'meat' content is suet!

Wedding cakes used to be called bride cakes or ring cakes. In Yorkshire it was an old custom to cut squares of the bride cake, throw them over the heads of the bride and groom and then put the pieces through the wedding ring. Sometimes it was broken over the bride's head and then thrown among the crowd to be scrambled for, or again, after being put through the wedding ring, pieces were put under guests' pillows at night to cause young people to dream of their lovers!

Many cakes take their name from royalty. Opposite the Royal Botanic Gardens at Kew stands a little teashop – the Maids of Honour. Maids of Honour cakes have been part of the history of Richmond, Surrey, for almost three hundred years. It is believed, however, that Henry VIII was the first to describe the cakes as such when he saw Anne Boleyn (1504–36) and other maids of honour eating the cakes from a silver dish. It appears he was so delighted with the cakes, and Anne, that he insisted the recipe was to be kept a royal secret and locked away in an iron box in Richmond Palace. However, by the early eighteenth century the recipe had somehow been made known to a Richmond baker, John Billet, who had a shop on the corner of Hill Street. It was here that Robert Newens served his apprenticeship. In 1850 he opened his premises in King Street, before later moving to 3 George Street where he continued the tradition of making and selling Maids of Honour. In 1887 Robert's son, Alfred, opened the present premises in Kew Road, taking with him the recipe for the delicious, small, puff-pastry tartlets, filled with a mixture of ground almonds, eggs and cream. The recipe is a family secret, but one which is undoubtedly enjoyed by the many visitors to Kew.

Another cake with royal connections is the Victoria sponge. After Prince Albert died, Queen Victoria spent much time at Osborne House on the Isle of Wight, and there started entertaining friends in the afternoon. Among the food served at these gatherings was a plain sponge, now often made with a jam and cream filling. The invention of baking powder in 1855 meant that there were great improvements in light cakes. This particular sponge eventually took Victoria's name.

Many tea-tables are enriched by a Battenberg cake, an

ABOVE LEFT: *The Maids of Honour shop in the eighteenth century.*
ABOVE RIGHT: *Anne Boleyn.*
RIGHT: *Queen Victoria.*
FACING PAGE, ABOVE: *Prince Henry of Battenberg.*

directly to 'Mountbatten', although the name of the cake remains unchanged.

The word biscuit is derived from the Latin *bis coctus*, meaning 'twice cooked' and has probably entered our language through the Old French *pain bescuit* – 'twice-cooked bread'. Whatever home-cooked, twice-baked biscuit offerings once existed, many of the biscuits we know and love today began to appear in the nineteenth century – probably as a result of growing opportunities for mass production.

In Queen Victoria's reign, biscuits, as cakes, were often introduced to commemorate royal occasions or famous personalities. The Osborne biscuit, for example, was named after Osborne House, on the Isle of Wight, which was purchased by Queen Victoria for the royal family in 1845. The biscuit was the creation of Francis Reckitt of Reckitt & Son, later Reckitt & Colman, in about 1860. They eventually sold their biscuit-making business goodwill to Peek Frean.

In the 1860s Peek Frean introduced the Nice biscuit, the name simply referring to their nice taste. However, most people linked the biscuit with Queen Victoria's trips to Nice in France, after a rumour that they were made specially to take abroad with her. Thus the pronunciation changed to 'Neece' and the biscuit continues to be called this.

One of Peek Frean's most famous biscuits, the Garibaldi, came on the market in 1861. It is said to be named after Giuseppe Garibaldi, the famous Italian exile and distinguished guerilla fighter and privateer, who became a hero in the eyes of the Italian people for his role in the 1859 war of Italian liberation. However, it is sometimes irreverently referred to as the

oblong sponge divided into four square sections, two coloured pink and two yellow, with a coating of jam and an outer wrap of marzipan. It is popularly believed that the four quarters honour the four handsome Battenberg princes, Louis, Alexander, Henry and Francis Joseph, and it is possible that the cake was first introduced to mark the occasion of Prince Louis' marriage to Princess Victoria of Hesse-Darmstadt, Queen Victoria's granddaughter. Prince Henry married Princess Beatrice, Queen Victoria's youngest child. Due to the war with Germany, King George V decided that the Royal house should anglicize its name; given the strength of anti-German feeling other leading families followed suit. Thus, in June 1917, the Battenberg family name was translated

'squashed fly' biscuit, owing to the appearance of the currants inside.

In 1875 Peek Frean also introduced the Marie biscuit in honour of the Grand Duchess Marie Alexandrovna of Russia, who, in 1874, had married Prince Alfred, Duke of Edinburgh – Queen Victoria's second son.

Mr Peek, a City tea merchant, had started a biscuit business for his two sons, and he appointed George Frean, a West Country miller, as its manager. The original Peek Frean factory was in Dockhead, near the

Thames in south-east London, but as early as 1924 a factory was established in India, others following in Australia and Canada. In 1902 Peek Frean launched the outstandingly successful Pat-a-Cake biscuit, a low-priced shortbread type of biscuit. Pat-a-Cakes were widely advertised in halfpenny magazines and elsewhere, and the manufacturer's delivery vans carried the slogan 'For goodness sake, eat Pat-a-Cake', the phrase becoming a catchword of the times. Peek Frean introduced the first chocolate-coated biscuit, Chocolate Table, in 1899 and the first chocolate-cream sandwich biscuit was introduced in 1910. Originally known as Creola, its name was changed to Bourbon a few months later, Bourbon being the name of the famous French family that for generations held the throne of France and Naples, and until 1931, that of Spain. Other cream biscuits followed such as Custard Creams and Lemon Puff Creams.

Cheeselets and Twiglets were developed by Peek Frean during the period between the two world wars, possibly because some people found it expensive to buy meat and cheese.

ABOVE FAR LEFT: *James Peek.*
ABOVE LEFT: *George Frean.*

BELOW LEFT:
Grand Duchess Marie Alexandrovna of Russia.

Certainly, during the Second World War the government encouraged people to eat more biscuits as a source of energy. Peek Frean went on to become part of Associated Biscuits Ltd, along with Huntley & Palmers and W. & R. Jacob & Co. Ltd. Today, as well as their many biscuits, they are now one of the major manufacturers of Christmas puddings.

In 1841 Thomas Huntley and George Palmer, cousins by marriage and both Quakers, became partners in a confectionery and biscuit-baking business in Reading. In 1846 they opened a fully-mechanized factory in King's Road, Reading, which enabled them to grow into a major player in the industry. They were later to become famous for their many highly-decorative biscuit tins, which are now collectors' items.

Richard and Joane Jacob, also Quakers, fled from the south-west of England to Ireland when the Quakers were being persecuted in

the late seventeenth century. It was descendants of this pair, brothers William and Robert Jacob, who began making 'fancy' biscuits at Waterford, a small town in Ireland in 1850. Later they moved to Dublin and it was from there that, in 1883, William Jacob's son, George, visited America. As a result of this visit the company started experimenting with crackers based on the American soda-type crackers. During 1885 the Cream Cracker – a name forever linked with Jacobs – was launched. Jacobs opened a Liverpool depot in 1886 and a factory at Aintree, outside Liverpool, in 1912.

Robert McVitie founded a high-quality retail bakery and confectionery business in Edinburgh's Rose Street in 1830. His son, also Robert, expanded the business, particularly developing the sale of biscuits to longer-distance customers. In 1887 Alexander Grant joined the firm, and in 1888 Charles Price, one of the McVitie salesmen, was made a partner, the company becoming McVitie and Price. George Andrews Brown, London and Southern Counties salesman for the company, is credited with the idea of making a sandwich biscuit with a cream filling, but it was Alexander Grant who, in 1892, created the recipe for the first Digestive biscuit. It has been made to almost exactly the same recipe ever since. The biscuit was originally called 'digestive' because it contains baking soda, which is known to help control flatulence – thus a product containing this 'medicinal' ingredient was felt to help digestion. It is said that Grant personally supervised the mixing of each batch of ingredients, the exact recipe being a tight secret. This sometimes meant that machines were kept idle until he came off the London to Edinburgh train. However, in the 1930s he passed this responsibility to his elder daughter, Elizabeth. Today about 6 million Digestives are eaten every day and McVitie's still makes at least half of them!

LEFT: *William Jacob.*

In 1939 McVitie's was manufacturing 370 different varieties of product, such as the Jaffa Cake which has been around for over 65 years. And they are still creating new brands – Hobnobs, for example, which, launched in 1986 and named after the 'hob' of a cooking stove and a 'nob' of butter, became a hit of the 1980s.

It was Macdonalds who, in 1946, launched a chocolate-covered, oblong-shaped, cream-filled sandwich biscuit, which they called Penguin. Penguin is regarded as a huge marketing success with its amusing packaging designs and advertisements, including the well-known phrase 'p-p-p-p-pick up a Penguin'. Macdonalds introduced Munchmallow in 1950 and YoYo, the chocolate-covered biscuit with a mint flavour, in 1954. The company was the first to abandon tinned biscuits in favour of individual packs that could be more easily accommodated on the counter. Later introductions were Bandit in 1959 and Taxi in 1960.

Macfarlane Lang, a family biscuit firm, were proud to be able to boast that Queen Victoria always had a tin of their Parmena biscuits

few years later they introduced 'assorted' shortbreads in round tins, which were an immediate success. In later years Crawford's lorries carried the slogan 'Crawford's Biscuits Are Best'. Interestingly, in his recent autobiography, the actor Michael Crawford admits that he took Crawford as his stage name because of a passing Crawford's lorry: 'One afternoon while walking down Sheerness High Street I saw a large biscuit lorry with an enormous sign along the side, reading "CRAWFORD'S Biscuits are Best." I don't know why, but the name jumped out at me.'

Simmers of Aberdeenshire, who have been baking shortbread for over a hundred years, are famous for their Petticoat Tails. This description may derive from the French expression *petites gatelles*, little scallops, referring to the scalloped edge of the shortbread, although it could also derive from *petites galettes*, little cakes. It is likely that the name

on her luncheon table, but the claim for the title of the oldest biscuit manufacturer (unless you can prove me wrong!) must go to Wm Crawford & Sons who commenced production in 1813 in a small shop in Leith, Edinburgh's famous port area. It was two of William Crawford's grandchildren, Archie and James, who built up the business in Liverpool's Binns Road (also famous as the home of Hornby trains). James Crawford was prepared to live frugally, but recognizing that selling was a vital ingredient of success, gave great importance to paying his salesmen (travellers) generously. And successful the company was. At one time James Crawford recorded that the area 'where the factory is being built gets six postal deliveries a day starting at 7.30 am'.

Shortbread has long been a national favourite in Scotland, but initially English folk did not take to the thick cakes. So, in 1904, the Crawford brothers started making thinner shortbreads at their factory in Liverpool. A

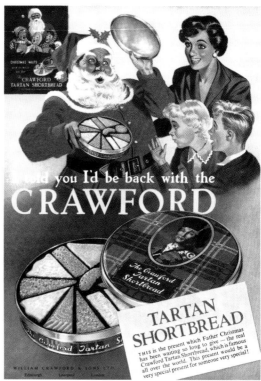

dates back to the reign of Mary Queen of Scots, as Mary had strong connections with France. Simmers, however, tell us that they prefer to believe Petticoat Tails are named after the bell-hoop petticoats worn by seventeenth-century court ladies, which shape they closely resemble.

The first biscuit manufacturer to receive a Royal Warrant was Carr's of Carlisle. Jonathan Dodgson Carr walked from Kendal to Carlisle in 1831 to seek his fortune. He set himself up as a baker in Castle Street and within three years he had also built a flourmill in Church Street. Among the provisions he sold were hand-made biscuits, and Queen Victoria granted him a Royal Warrant for these in 1841. The company was also the first to install biscuit-cutting machinery. Inspired by the hand-operated printing press he saw at the firm that made his biscuit tins, Carr got the idea for a machine to cut biscuits. It was this machine that shaped the first Alphabet biscuits, so loved by young children for generations.

The word 'cookie' comes from the Dutch *koekje*, which means a small cake rather than a reference to cooking. The first cookies to be introduced in the United Kingdom, in 1956,

Issued by the Cake and Biscuit Manufacturers War Time Alliance to remind you that biscuits simply cannot be beaten as a compact energy food.

girls would take the biscuits, a bowl of cheese (with an additive to give it spreadability) and a special knife. The girls then handspread the biscuits and wrapped them. The company also introduced the idea of packaging cheese and biscuits wrapped in foil.

Savoury biscuit snacks became increasingly popular. The German pretzel is one such snack, but not many people know that pretzels were first baked by medieval monks to be used as rewards for children learning holy lessons. The pretzel is shaped to represent a pair of arms folded in prayer across a child's chest.

In 1926 Campbell Garatt started to import crispbread from Sweden, where rye flour was being used to make characteristic dark bread. Each year, at the end of the harvest, large quantities of dark, firm bread were baked into crisp, thin disks, with a hole at the centre. The

were Maryland Cookies, manufactured by Symbol Biscuits, a subsidiary of J Lyons & Co Ltd. New biscuit-making technology introduced from the United States enabled the inclusion of 'choc chips' into biscuit dough, which remained intact during baking. This was a major breakthrough in biscuit making. While Maryland Cookies are still a winning brand, the world's bestselling cookie is the Oreo, made by Nabisco Brands. The first Oreo was sold in New Jersey in 1912 and in the United States over 6 billion are sold each year.

When the firms of Meredith and Drew came together, it was the toss of a coin that decided the order of the two names. Meredith & Drew Ltd came into being in 1891, some sixty years after William Meredith started as a baker in London. The company became renowned for their cheese biscuits, at one time advertising them as 'A meal for a penny'. In the early years of the twentieth century their Cheddar Sandwich was made in their London factory, where

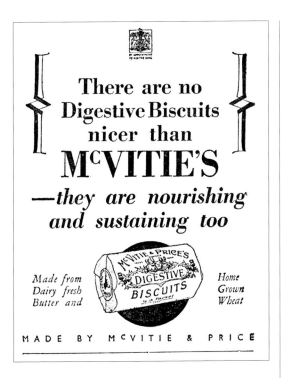

There are no
Digestive Biscuits
nicer than
McVITIE'S
—*they are nourishing*
and sustaining too

Made from
Dairy fresh
Butter and

Home
Grown
Wheat

MADE BY McVITIE & PRICE

south coast, and Garfield Weston then bought the company – he later became chairman of Associated British Foods plc. Ryvita was granted a Royal Warrant in 1950 by King George VI, an honour that continues today.

The familiar Ryvita dimples are made by spiked 'dockering' rollers, the purpose being to increase the surface area, which is essential to ensure the exact crispbake texture and flavour, whilst the process also helps to 'pin' the top and bottom surfaces together. The company entered the 'extrusion' market (where the mixture is forced out of tubes before being baked) when they introduced Crackerbread in 1979, and now also manufacture a range of extruded cereals.

The vast range of cakes and biscuits we have on our shelves continues to grow, especially now supermarkets have 'own brand' products. Nutritionists tell us that too many are bad for us – but sometimes there's nothing better than a favourite cake or biscuit when we're feeling a little peckish.

disks were then strung on to a pole where they continued to dry and were used throughout the winter. These are the original versions of our modern crispbreads.

The Ryvita company was established in 1930 and soon afterwards it set up its own bakery in Birmingham. An adjoining mill provided the company's flour, but war damage closed the plant and the production was taken over by Rowntree. After the war Ryvita was produced at new plants in Poole, on the

Fresh from the Sea
FISH & SHELLFISH

Our ancestors followed religious practices more rigidly than some of us do today – including religious instructions on the consumption of food. In medieval times it was a religious tradition that fish was eaten during Lent and on fast-days when meat was forbidden. In 1564 Elizabeth I pronounced Wednesday a fish day, ostensibly in support of the fishing industry but also as an anti-Catholic gesture – the Catholic Church long having observed Fridays as a day of abstinence, which meant that meat was not permitted.

There has been a great variety of fish eaten in Britain for many centuries. Records show that, when people still believed they were fish, whales, porpoise, grampus, and sea wolf were allowed to be eaten during Lent. In 1246 Henry III asked the sheriffs of London to purchase 100 pieces of whale for his table and the British Museum has a manuscript for making 'puddyings of porpoise', which was on the menu at the table of King Henry VIII!

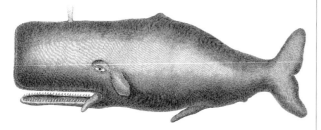

Nor was the eating of fish limited to coastal towns. To ensure a regular supply of fish, stew-ponds were attached to manor houses and monasteries, and moats around castles were stocked with luce,

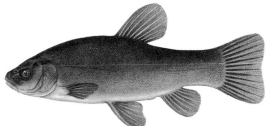

pike, carp or tench. There was also a strong merchant trade between coastal towns and large inland settlements. In one year during the reign of King Edward III (1312–77), the royal household was supplied with five lasts of red herrings, two lasts of white herrings, two barrels of sturgeon, 1,300 stockfish (dried cod), 89 congers and 320 mulwells.

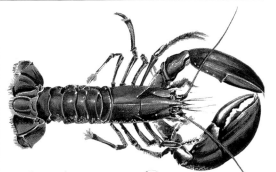

The town of Yarmouth in Norfolk has been associated with bloaters and red herrings since as far back as the fifth century. In fact the herring was the reason that the town came into existence. As shoals left the open seas near to what is now Scarborough, they swam southwards down the coast, past Grimsby, until they reached the waters around Suffolk. The site of the town was originally a sandbank in the sea, generally covered by the waves. However, at some point in the fifth century it became a permanent landmass and fishermen found it was a convenient place to dry the nets they were using to catch their fish. Gradually a trade in herrings grew from here and merchants would come from Norwich and even London to transact business. Buildings were erected on the site and a seaside town began to grow.

Even royalty considered herring pies to be a delicacy. Great Yarmouth was required by ancient charter to send to the king each year a hundred herrings baked in 24 pies or pasties. In the reign of Edward I, Eustace de Corson, Thomas de Berkedich and Robert de Withen were each given thirty acres of land in return for supplying the king with 24 pasties of fresh herrings on their first coming into season.

The herring season lasts eighteen to twenty weeks. Traditionally, as the fish were taken from their nets, they were cast into the hold of the fishing boat where layers of fish were alternated with a covering of salt: one ton of salt to each last of fish. The term 'last' nominally means 12 barrels or ten thousand fish, but in fact it is thirteen thousand two hundred as, according to the unusual computation of the fishers, one hundred and thirty-two fish were counted as a hundred. An ordinary fishing boat would hold from twenty to twenty-five

FACING PAGE: *Great sturgeon, sperm whale, tench, conger eel, unknown.*
ABOVE: *Herring.*
ABOVE RIGHT: *Lobster.*
RIGHT: *Salting herrings in 1905.*

De Halece , ſiue Arenga

LEFT: *A fisherman with a fine catch of herrings in 1555.*

lasts, the boat sometimes being filled by one cast of the nets. The herrings were taken from the boats to the premises of the curers where women washed them in huge tubs. They were then transferred to long sticks, which were poked through the eyes of the herrings, and the sticks were then hung from beams in smokehouses. Some of the fish were removed after an hour or two – these are known as bloaters, whereas those fish remaining longer in the smokehouse became red or black herrings, depending on the length of curing.

Black herrings were predominantly exported to Catholic countries. Certainly, in Britain, we are more familiar with the red variety – or perhaps it is just with the saying 'It's a red herring', meaning something that diverts atten-

tion away from what one is seeking. The expression may well derive from dog training, as dog-trainers learned long ago that red herring has a peculiarly persistent smell and thus it is easy for a dog to follow its scent. The author of *The Gentleman's Recreation*, 1686, advised that if a dog could not be trained by dragging a dead cat or a dead fox, a red herring, having a more powerful smell, should be used. However, this failsafe procedure could also be used for leading a dog on a false trail, the smell of the herring being so powerful that the dog would lose any other scent he had been following. Criminals being chased by bloodhounds could therefore use this to their advantage. There is also an expression in our language, 'Neither fish, flesh, nor good red herring', meaning something that is of no purpose to anyone. It dates from a time when fish was regarded as food for the clergy, meat was for people with money, and the common herring was for the poor.

From about the 1820s, herrings that would normally have been sold fresh at local markets went for 'kippering'. This method of preserving the fish entailed them being packed overnight in coarse-grained salt before being arranged on sticks in the smokehouse over smouldering oak-chips, which gradually turned them into the coppery colour we expect kippers to be. There are many fishing towns we can associate with kippers, Whitby being among them. Loch Fyne kippers are a particularly well-known Scottish delicacy, and the Loch Fyne company claims that they are served for breakfast in all leading European hotels.

Bismarck herrings and rollmops are the whole sides of herrings with the bones

RIGHT: *Salting, drying and smoking fish in 1555.*
BELOW LEFT: *Salmon.*
BELOW RIGHT: *Trawler fishermen haul in their nets.*

De Pifcibus falfis, ficcatis, & fumigatis.

removed. They are uncooked, but pickled in a spiced vinegar and flavoured with bay leaves, red peppers and herbs. Rollmops are generally rolled around some onion hence the 'roll'. The name is actually of German origin, however, from *rollen*, 'to roll', and *mops*, meaning 'pug dog' – a dubious reference, perhaps, to their appearance. Herring roes are often to be found in fish hors d'oeuvres along with sardines and anchovies.

It is said that salmon were once so plentiful in the river Thames that even the poor turned their noses up at them. However, today, as at other times in history, this fish is regarded as something of a luxury. You still sometimes see the name 'salmon trout' on fishmongers' stalls and restaurant menus. In fact this is a more glamorous name for the common sea trout. This 'deception' dates from the days before trout and salmon farming became widespread, but when wild trout stocks were plentiful and thus cheap. Salmon, however, being a migratory fish and subject to all sorts of

problems that can reduce stocks in any given year, was more expensive. As the two fish are both pink-fleshed from feeding on ocean shrimp, it was tempting for people to pass off

the trout as the more desirable salmon. In fact the trout is every bit as delicious – especially when smoked. Scotland is famous for both smoked salmon and smoked trout and exports them throughout the world – from places like Tobermory on the Isle of Mull to as far away as the United States.

Chambers's Journal of 1880 records details of how the first salmon were introduced into

1.—Red Mullet.   2.—Grayling.   3.—John Dory.   4.—Mackerel.   5.—Cod.   6.—Whiting.   7.—Salmon.   8.—Herring.   9.—Plaice.   10.—Flounder.   11.—Gurnet.   12.—Crayfish.

ABOVE LEFT: *Brown trout.*
FACING PAGE, LEFT: *Brown crab and native oyster.*
FACING PAGE, RIGHT: *Whitstable oyster boat at sea.*

Australia. After several failed attempts to transport salmon eggs to the antipodean colony, on 21 January 1864 four thousand salmon ova left England for Melbourne, some 15,000 miles away, and were safely shipped to shore on 15 April. Of these, four hundred hatched in the nursery on the River Plenty – the start of a great industry. *Chambers's Journal* also reports that, in 1898, 22 adult trout, of an average weight of five pounds, were brought to London on the steamship *Otarama*. Five weeks earlier

the trout had been swimming in one of New Zealand's rivers. They were in fact making a return journey, the trout having been raised from ova sent from Britain.

Cromer, on the north-Norfolk coast, is renowned for its crabs. The fishing ground around Cromer is a rocky area extending about twenty miles along the coast and about four miles out from the shore. Although there are other landing points within that area, all the catch are called Cromer crabs. The crabs are caught in 'pots', a type of basket also used to catch lobsters, and which were first used in about 1860.

Colchester, in Essex, has been known for its oysters since Roman times. In 1196 Richard I granted the Corporation of Colchester rights to the oyster beds, which are actually some miles away from the town, where the river Colne runs into the estuary at Brightlingsea. Each September, the mayor and the town's councillors still open the oyster-dredging season, in full ceremonial regalia. They set sail for the oyster-fattening beds in Pyfleet where the town clerk reads out a proclamation and the mayor lowers the first oyster dredge. Each October the Corporation holds an Oyster Feast in Colchester's Moot Hall.

Whilst its boatbuilding, shrimping industry and 'Crab & Winkle Line' railway to Canterbury have now disappeared, Whitstable in Kent is

then at the over-fishing of the seas and the netting of immature fish, and a Select Committee of the House of Commons was already making an inquiry into the state of our fishing areas. Hatcheries had been established in Scotland, Canada, Norway and the United States of America, where sea fishes could be reared, and it was anticipated that by the end of that year 30 million young 'fry' would be released into the waters of the Firth of Forth.

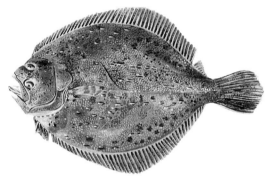

also famous for its oysters – as well as for other seafoods such as whelks and cockles. The people of Whitstable have long made a trade from the sea. In Saxon times there are records of salt workings, and the Domesday Book records three manorial centres at Seasalter with eight fisheries. In 1312 fishermen were allowed to sell their catches toll free at Canterbury market and in 1480 Whitstable fish-market was created, which survived until the nineteenth century. In 1793 the Oyster Company of Free Fishers and Dredgers was set up by local fishermen and flourished for many years. However, the success of the oyster beds was diminished by the First World War and in the 1920s a parasitic disease, which practically wiped out the Whitstable Native oyster, devastated the oyster beds. After this, the hardier Pacific or rock oyster was mainly cultivated, but even these fared badly when, in 1963, the sea froze for up to a mile offshore for ten weeks. However, oysters continue to be a Whitstable speciality to this day and are well worth making a trip to the town for.

In 1894 Grimsby was the largest and most important fishing port in the world with a fleet of 819 vessels, made up of 695 trawlers and 124 cod vessels. Almost 5,000 men formed their crews, catching 74,000 tons of fish a year – a mix of haddock, plaice, sole, turbot and halibut. Concern was being expressed even

Low fishstocks were the reason for the 'Cod War' – the name given to an extended period of tension between Britain and Iceland over

FAR LEFT: *Whitstable fishermen come ashore with their catch of oysters.*
LEFT: *Turbot.*
RIGHT: *Scottish fishergirls working at Scarborough.*
BELOW LEFT: *Cod.*
BELOW RIGHT: *Lemon sole.*

the latter's extension of her fishing limits. The reason for this is that the main cod shoals are found off Newfoundland and Iceland, and by the 1950s cod stocks were already running low. In 1959 Icelandic gunboats fired live ammunition at British trawlers, and in 1972 sank two of them. Royal Navy frigates were sent on several occasions to protect British vessels fishing in Icelandic waters, and there were a number of times when these fired warning shots across the bows of Icelandic gunboats – said to be the first time the navy had fired its guns in anger since the Korean War.

Whitby is another ancient and famous fishing port situated between the North York Moors and the North Sea at the mouth of the River Esk. Among its famous sea-faring sons are Captain James Cook, the eighteenth-century explorer, and the men of the Scoresby family who were famous whalemasters in their day. Whitby was once the main whaling port for the North of England before the overhunting of whales led to restrictions and bans.

Sometimes the names of fish can be misleading. Bombay duck, for example, is in fact the bummalo fish, which is sold dried and packed in cartons. Lemon sole would suggest either that the fish is a lemon-yellow colour or that it is flavoured with lemon. However, it is likely that its name stems from the fact that the sole swims along the sea-bed and therefore the word 'lemon' may come from the Latin word *limus*, meaning mud. Alternatively, 'lemon' may refer to the sole being a flat fish, a translation from the French *limande* which is used to describe any kind of flat fish.

A truly yellow-coloured fish is Finnan haddock, the colour resulting from smoking the fish over green wood. The name Finnan haddock was originally Findhorn haddock, named after the port of Findhorn, near Aberdeen in Scotland. It is said that the spots on the body of

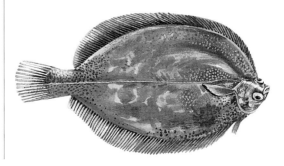

the fish, just behind the pectoral fins, were caused by the finger and thumb of St Peter, the fisherman apostle. Supposedly it is the had-

dock that is referred to in St Matthew's Gospel, when Jesus told Peter to draw a fish from the water and that in its mouth he would find a coin sufficient to pay the temple tax.

shrimp is *scampo*, the plural is *scampi*. Therefore any serving of shrimps could be called 'scampi'. To confuse matters further, large shrimps are also called prawns.

Similar marks are found on the John Dory. The John Dory is a golden-yellow fish whose name is said to derive from the French words *jaune*, meaning yellow, and *dorée*, meaning gold or 'gilded one'. However, in France it is known only as *la dorée*, and there is a possibility that the word 'John' was added much later. It is a member of the mackerel family and is common both in Mediterranean waters and around the coasts of south-west England. In France it is also known as *Le poisson de St Pierre*, again because of the marks near the pectoral fins.

Confusion also occurs between shrimps, scampi and prawns. The Italian word for a

Sturgeon and caviar have long been associated with royalty and the homes of the rich. The sturgeon, often described as a 'curious monster of the deep', is a fish particularly associated with Russian waters. Historically, when it was found in British waters it was claimed by the monarch and made into a pie to grace the royal table. A large sturgeon may measure up to 7 feet in length, and one particularly large one caught not far from the mouth of the Ural weighed 2,520 lbs! Caviar is the name given to the roe of the sturgeon after it has been prepared for market, and is generally seasoned

TOP LEFT: *Haddock.*
TOP RIGHT: *Lobster.*
ABOVE LEFT: *John Dory.*
ABOVE RIGHT: *Prawn.*
FACING PAGE, ABOVE LEFT: *Fishermen removing caviar from sturgeon in Astrakhan, Russia in 1913.*

'chippy' was a Mr Lees who sold fish and chips from a wooden hut in the market at Oldham in 1863. Today there are about nine thousand fish and chip shops throughout Britain, the most

with oil, vinegar or lemon juice and served on toasted bread. Captain Burnaby, in his book *Ride to Khiva*, recommends that 'a little pressed or fresh caviar, and a glass or so of Russian vodka, taken before sitting down to dinner, give a wonderful stimulus to the appetite'. He also suggests that sturgeon, served in cold slices with jelly and horseradish sauce, is not to be despised. Beluga is the name given to the larger white sturgeon and it is this fish that is the usual source of caviar.

The origins of Fish and Chips seem to have been lost in the passage of time, but some suggest that the process of battering and frying fish was brought to London by the Sephardic Jews, who settled in London's East End in the late eighteenth century – they having developed their fish-frying skills during an earlier stay in Spain. In 1839 when Charles Dickens was writing *Oliver Twist*, he mentions a fried-fish warehouse.

In 1860 Oliver Malin opened something called a 'fish and chip shop' in Cleveland Street in the City of London. The north's first

famous one being Harry Ramsden's at White Cross, Guiseley, near Leeds, which attracts local people and celebrities alike.

Harry Ramsden was the son of a fish and chip man, but set up on his own after the First World War in a lock-up shop on the outskirts of Bradford. However, Harry's wife Beatrice suffered from tuberculosis and Harry was advised by her doctor to move to the country where the air was clean and fresh. Thus, in 1928, they moved to a little cottage in White Cross. Harry, then 42 years old, borrowed £150 to open a new shop in Guiseley. The business started modestly but, whether Harry knew it or not, he had chosen the ideal location for his fish and chip shop, for it was on the direct route for people travelling from the cities of Leeds and Bradford to the Lake District, as well as to Blackpool, Morecambe and the Yorkshire Dales. Harry also delivered fish and chips to nearby

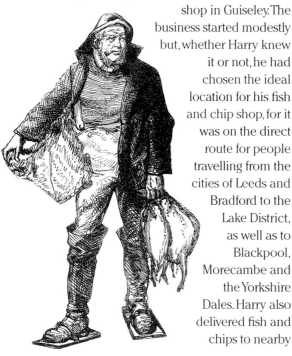

factories and other large employers – all of which helped to expand his business. Harry then embarked on an ambitious plan to build the largest fish and chip emporium in the country. He borrowed two thousand pounds each from his potato dealer, his fish supplier and his fat supplier, and by 1931 Harry Ramsden's was ready for business.

Sadly, Beatrice had died the year after their move to the country and was therefore never to see the magnificent restaurant with its beautiful leaded windows, lights and carpeting. Such was the splendour of 'Harry Ramsden's' that it prompted one young lad to ask his father, 'Is this where God comes for his fish and chips?'

FACING PAGE, ABOVE RIGHT: *The symbol of Macfisheries.*
RIGHT: *Harry Ramsden's luxury fish restaurant at White Cross.*
BELOW LEFT: *Harry Ramsden outside his original shop.*

However glamorous his restaurant, Harry kept in mind that his food was not just for the well-to-do and this paid off during the years of the 1930s Depression. When most households had little money left at the end of the week, fish and chips provided a cheap meal – a fish costing 2d and chips a penny!

Today the grandeur of Harry Ramsden's is still maintained, but it is also possible to enjoy their fish and chips in other parts of Britain and abroad – in Blackpool, Manchester, Hong Kong and even as far away as Melbourne, Australia.

Perhaps the best-known seller of wet fish was Macfisheries, who opened their first shop in 1919 and by the end of 1921 had 360 shops. However, as the fishing fleets were reduced, and frozen fish became available, fewer house-wives bought wet fish and gradually the firm went into decline – but its memory lives on in many families.

Fish is still a staple part of our diet – whether it is fish and chips or the more exotic

sushi, shark steaks or swordfish, which we can now buy in our local fishmongers and supermarkets. Canning and freezing of fish (see *Making It Last*) may have led to most of the household products we find in our kitchen cupboards and fridge-freezers today, but for many people fresh is best. British ports such as Newquay, Morecambe, Falmouth, Fishguard, Oban, Mallaig, Tobermory and Fleetwood still have flourishing fish industries, and local fish restaurants illustrate the many exquisite ways we can enjoy the magnificent harvest of our rivers and seas.

A Sweet Tooth
SWEETS & CHOCOLATES

Most of the traditional brands of sweets and chocolate goodies on our shelves today have their origins in the last two hundred years. However, sweets and chocolate have been around for a long, long time, and there is evidence to suggest that people of ancient civilizations had a tooth every bit as sweet as ours.

Archaeologists have found evidence of confectionery being made by the Egyptians

Cadbury's Cocoa is pure; do not take or give your children foreign preparations mixed with Alkali.

CADBURY'S
Chocolate
EASTER EGGS

over 3,500 years ago, and Egyptian hieroglyphics dating as far back as the sixteenth century BC show us that honey-based sweets and chopped fruits were available in the market place. These sweetmeats appear to have been crude in shape and highly coloured.

Although the Romans had discovered how to make sugared almonds – by coating nuts with sugar and adding successive layers of sugar syrup until a hard outer shell is formed – Ancient Britons seem to have had few of the ingredients we use in confectionery making today. Honey, however, was widely used both as a sweetener and as a preservative (honey discourages the growth of bacteria and therefore slows down decay); hence honey refining was an important part of domestic life.

FREE *to users of Rowntree's Cocoa and Table Jellies*

Much reduced illustration

ROWNTREE'S FREE GIFT CASKET

With its gay design in bright colours of gardens and flowers, Rowntree's Free Gift Casket is a representation of the popular raffia work, reproduced in the best style on metal. It is decorative. It is useful. It has two layers of delicious chocolates and confectionery. And you get it "double quick." Rowntree's Cocoa *and* Table Jellies contain coupons.

Start collecting from both to-day and see over for particulars.

Honeycomb and sweetened fruit and nuts might well be the nearest to confectionery our ancestors came. However, records show that by the thirteenth century sugar was being used in confectionery making in Europe. In about 1200 a chemist living in Verdun created a sweetmeat by coating almonds with a mixture of sugar and honey, which sounds very similar to dragées. In 1407 marchpane (marzipan) was being made in the Baltic cities of Lübeck and Königsberg, as well as in cities in France and Italy. Sugared almonds were introduced to France in 1600. In 1701 the Duc de Bourgogne and the Duc de Berry were presented with a gift of white nougat by the citizens of Montéli-mar. Praline, a confection of nuts and caramelized sugar, was first dished up by the chef to the Comte de Plessis-Praslin (1598–1675), hence its name. Caramel was known in Turkey and other eastern Mediter-ranean countries. Immigrants to North America introduced it there in the nineteenth century, although it was not manufactured in Britain until 1883.

The ingredient we associate most with confectionery is, of course, sugar. Sugar comes from two sources, from sugar cane, *Saccharum officinarum*, and sugar-beet, *Beta vulgaris*. More

Bunodes gemmacea.

than two thousand years ago Indian farmers were growing sugar cane and knew how to produce sugar crystals. Those living on the border with China sent part of their crop to the Chinese Emperor as a way of keeping the peace, and, subsequently, Emperor Tai Tsung sent people to India to discover how this highly-desirable substance was obtained. By the thirteenth century the Chinese had a large number of sugar factories, although there is no evidence that they were making hard-boiled sweets. People in Indonesia also shared this knowledge, and it is possible that we get the word 'sugar' from the Indonesian word *shekar*. However, it may also derive from the Persian *shakar* or from Sanskrit *sarkarà*.

It is not known when sugar first made its way to Britain, although certainly by the thirteenth century the word *suker* had entered the English language. In *Our English Home*, of 1876, James Parker tells us that in 1226 Henry III asked the Mayor of Winchester to get him 3 lbs of sugar of Alexandria, if it could be found among the merchants of the city. It wasn't until the time of the Crusades that sugar was generally introduced to Britain, when, along with spices, plants and other new goods, returning soldiers brought it back with them from abroad. Even so, it is likely that until the sugar plantations were developed in the West Indies and sugar was shipped to Britain, honey remained the main sweetener in most households.

In 1747 a German chemist called Andreas Sigismund Marggraf discovered that sugar could be easily extracted from beet. In France,

the development of this industry was encouraged by Napoleon, while the English beet industry did not begin commercial production until 1921 when two factories were built in East Anglia.

Sugar boiling started in Kendal in 1700, and boiled sweets, toffees and Black Bull's Eyes

have all been made there. Of course, the confectionery for which the town is best known is Kendal Mint Cake, a white, crystallized sugar bar, which in the past has been highly regarded as a source of energy. Kendal Mint Cake was among the provisions that Captain Scott took with him on his 1912 expedition to the South Pole. Sir Edmund Hillary also had some with him on his successful climb to the summit of Mount Everest in May 1953. Hence the Kendal Mint Cake is among the world's most travelled sweets. Kendal Mint Cake is thought to have been made first by Joseph Wiper at the end of the nineteenth century. He, however, left England for Canada in 1913, leaving the business to his nephew. About this time other companies also caught on to the sweet's popularity. Wilson's commenced production in 1913 and Quiggin's in 1920. Joseph Wiper's original business was taken over by George Romney Ltd in 1937 – all are still in existence.

If we go to the seaside for the day or for a holiday it has been traditional to bring back a stick of rock. A man named Ben Bullock, who originally came from Burnley in Lancashire, made the first Blackpool Rock in 1887 – probably in Dewsbury in Yorkshire. Bullock had been making rock with letters through it for about twenty years, but it was while he was on holiday in Blackpool that he realized the potential for selling sticks of rock in the popular sea-side resort. Other early manufacturers of rock were John Bull at Bridlington and Brown's of Cleethorpes. Rock is basically made from sugar and water, with liquid glucose added to prevent the sugar crystallizing. The ingredients are boiled for about 15 minutes in special copper pans, during which most of the water evaporates. The mixture is then poured on to water-cooled tables, where it is allowed to reduce in temperature. Next it is divided into two parts, one of which is kept clear and is transferred to a 'pulling machine', to aerate it (it is the presence of air which makes the rock white). Colouring and flavouring are added to the other part, the traditional pink and peppermint being the most popular. The batches are then recombined and are pulled by hand until the rock forms strings, which are cut into lengths ready for wrapping. The whole process is a skilled job.

Everton Toffee originated in the middle of the eighteenth century – in a small cottage in the village of Everton on the outskirts of Liverpool. Mrs Molly Bushell was encouraged to take up toffee making by her doctor, who was in the habit of recommending toffee to his patients as a cure for sore throats, coughs and colds. Molly herself does not seem to have suffered from such symptoms – rather she had impressed the doctor with her aptitude for hard work and the way in which she made slender means go a long way. The doctor gave Molly a good recipe and spread the word about her toffee making.

TOP LEFT AND RIGHT: *Early post-card advertisements for Fry's Five Boys chocolate and the rarer Five Girls.* BELOW LEFT: *The original Everton Toffee shop.*

Thus Molly's business began to take off. Everton, at this time, was a place where the well-to-do lived and a visiting place for tourists. Seeing that she had a good market for her toffee, Molly set up a small shop in the village, at No 1 Browside, although it is disputed whether or not this is the shop shown in the advertisements for Everton Toffee. On her death in 1818, her son-in-law, John Cooper, continued the business.

Moving on to the land of the White Rose, Pontefract has long had an association with liquorice. In the eleventh century Cluniac monks from France established a monastery in the town and found that liquorice plants,

which they had brought with them, grew well in the deep soils of the area – an extract from the plant's roots being used for medicinal purposes. In fact its medicinal properties were known even before Christ. A substantial amount of liquorice was found in Tutankhamen's tomb, and the healing effects of the liquorice root are

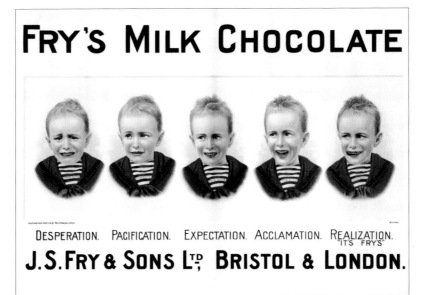

told about in Egyptian hieroglyphics. The cultivation of liquorice (*Glycyrrhiza glabra*) in England became quite widespread throughout the Middle Ages, and after the dissolution of the monasteries local farmers continued to grow the plants.

There are records that show that in 1614 liquorice lozenges were being manufactured to ease stomach disorders. George Dunhill, a Pontefract chemist, produced the first liquorice sweet by mixing the root with wheat flour and sugar, which not only made it taste nicer but made it last longer. In the 1760s he made the first Pomfret cake, 'Pomfret' being the

old name for Pontefract, although these early sweetmeats were also known as Yorkshire Pennies because of their origin and round shape. Other local people started to manufacture liquorice products. One of the first was John Hillaby, who set up business around 1850. By 1890 he had the largest liquorice manufactory in the world. Pomfret cakes were his main product, but he had also patented liquorice and malt lozenges, liquorice wafers, voice tablets and Hillaby's Lion juice. A large percentage of his products were exported to various parts of the world.

Another well known name in Pontefract was W. R. Wilkinson. He started out with a simple

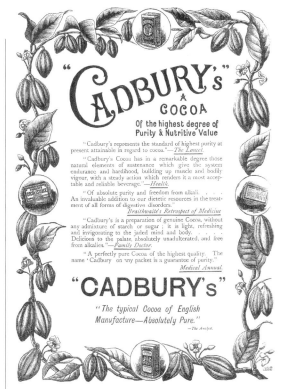

malt kiln, but today his original company is part of the Trebor Bassett group, based in Sheffield, who still produce Pontefract Cakes, as well as other well-loved liquorice sweets such as Catherine Wheels, bootlaces, Wilko Mints and liquorice pipes.

George Bassett was born at Ashover, near Chesterfield, in 1818. When he was only twelve his father died, and at the age of fourteen he was apprenticed to a confectioner and fruiterer. Ten years later he had become a wholesale confectioner, lozenge maker and British wine dealer. In 1858 he moved his firm to premises in Portland Street in Sheffield, where they made lozenges, pastilles, liquorice, acid drops, candied peel, orange marmalade, comfits and jujubes, which were sold throughout Britain and also overseas. Bassett's is still best known for its Liquorice Allsorts and the story of their origin has been often retold. In 1899 Charlie Thompson, a Bassett traveller, was selling his products to a wholesaler in

and South America. Likewise, the Ancient Greeks, especially women, chewed mastic gum – pronounced mas-tee-ka – as a way of cleaning their teeth and sweetening their breath. This gum is obtained from the bark of the mastic tree, which grows in Greece and Turkey. The word 'mastic' is related to our word 'masticate', meaning to chew.

Today chewing gum is made up of a mixture of edible latexes (of which chicle is still the best known), sugar, corn syrup, softeners (refined vegetable-oil products) and flavours. The sapodilla tree must be at least thirty years old to produce a good yield of chicle. A native worker, called a chiclero, climbs the tree and cuts grooves in the trunk, feeding the liquid inside into a container at the base of the tree. The latex is then heated until it

Leicester. At that time the different types of liquorice sweets were sold separately. Unfortunately, during the course of his presentation, Charlie knocked over his sample boxes and the sweets fell together on to the counter and got mixed up. However, the customer liked the look of the mixture Charlie was now presenting to him – hence the first sale of Liquorice Allsorts. Among the liquorice sweets for which the company is also famous is the Sherbert Fountain.

Some people are under the misapprehension that chewing gum was invented in the United States. It has certainly been heavily promoted and publicized by Americans, but chewing gum has an ancient history. The Mayas, an ancient American-Indian people and neighbours of the Aztecs, chewed chicle – a gumlike substance that is still the main ingredient in chewing gum – over a thousand years ago. Chicle is obtained from the milky juice or latex of the sapodilla tree (*Achras sapota*), which grows in the tropical rain forests of Central

Would you take a glass-and-a-half of milk on the golf links? You might be glad of it half-way through the game, especially if it was in the handy form of Cadburys Dairy Milk Chocolate. Did *you* know there's a glass-and-a-half of full-cream dairy milk in every half-pound block?

Marvellous that anything so nice can be so full of real goodness too. But, as you see, Mars bars are packed with all those good things that nourish, energise and sustain you.

milk chocolate coating.
caramel layer of sugar, malt, glucose and milk.
delicious centre of malt, chocolate, glucose and sugar — all whipped in white of egg.

thickens, at which point it is poured into moulds that hold about 25 lbs of the substance. These are then carried on pack mules out of the jungle to be flown to manufacturing plants.

The best known name in chewing gum production is that of William Wrigley Jr. William Wrigley moved to Chicago in 1891, at the age of 29, with only $32 in his pocket and a burning ambition to start a business of his own. Wrigley had unlimited energy and enthusiasm and proved to have great talent as a salesman. At first he sold soap to wholesalers, stimulating sales by offering free gifts with each purchase. One of these premiums was baking powder, but when this proved more popular than the soap he switched to selling baking powder instead. In 1892 Wrigley started offering two packets of chewing gum with each can of baking powder. The offer was a great success – but again the free gift was proving more popular than the item it was supposed to be promoting.

There were then about a dozen chewing gum companies in the United States, but Wrigley soon knew this was the market he would corner. That year he produced two new brands of gum – Lotta and Vassar – and in 1893 he launched Juicy Fruit and Wrigley's Spearmint. Several of the other gum companies merged to form 'the chewing gum trust', creating great competition for smaller players. However, Wrigley persevered, pioneering advertising and maximizing his undoubted skills of salesmanship. He decided to concentrate on Wrigley's Spearmint, which, although Wrigley himself believed it to be a superior product, was proving a slow seller. In 1906 he started to promote it through advertising and by 1910 it was America's favourite brand. Wrigley's started to open other factories outside America – including their first factory in Great Britain in 1927. Outside America the pellet-shaped P. K. Chewing Gum, which was introduced in a tightly-sealed pack, rather than loose in a box, soon became another Wrigley's market leader. In fact the product's name comes from its packaging – *P*acked tight – *K*ept right!

Chocolate was known in Central and Southern America long before the Spanish and Portuguese conquerors arrived there. The Aztec term for the drink was *Xocoatl*, which was translated by the Spanish as 'chocolate'. It is said that the word sounds like that of the clattering sound made by the native handmill used to grind the cocoa and mix it with sugar. In Prescott's *Conquest of Peru* we are told:

BELOW: *William Wrigley.*

…the emperor took no other beverage than the chocolate, a potation of chocolate with vanilla and other spices, so prepared as to be reduced to a froth of a consistency of honey, which gradually dissolved in the mouth and was taken cold, served in golden goblets and spoons.

We are also told that the emperor had no fewer than fifty jars or pitchers for his own daily use.

Like liquorice and toffee, chocolate was used for medicinal purposes. In 1519 a Spanish explorer, Don Cortez, conquered Mexico and brought cocoa beans back to Spain, and in 1591 a Spanish doctor published a book on chocolate's healing powers.

When cocoa was first brought to France, the Paris faculty of medicine endorsed it with much enthusiasm. However, when the French authorities got to hear claims of chocolate's aphrodisiac properties, their enthusiasm gave way to suspicion.

The first chocolate-based drinks were served as homage to Spanish conquerors, but were rather bitter and were not enjoyed by Europeans until they had been adapted to suit our tastebuds. Chocolate, as a drink, was introduced into England in the 1650s and the first 'chocolate house' opened in London in Bishopgate Street, in Queen's Head Alley, in

1657. It remained a luxury which only the very rich could afford; ladies would sip their chocolate at Don Saltero's in Chelsea, while the men frequented such fashionable gathering places as the Cocoa Tree, White's and the St James's, these later becoming gentlemen's clubs.

Gradually the popularity of chocolate spread. Mrs Elizabeth Montagu, 'the Queen of Blue Stockings', wrote from Bath to her friend Mrs Vesey: 'We take our chocolate every day at the pump-room. It is the best I have ever tasted. There is nothing like it in London.'

Cocoa had become popular in Bristol by 1702 and chocolate houses stood side by side with spirit shops on the Clifton Downs. Walter Churchman opened his cocoa-drink processing plant in Bristol in 1728, which thirty years later was taken over by Joseph Fry, founder of Fry & Sons. About the middle of the eighteenth century the *Bristol Journal* announced, 'Mr Joseph Fry is removed from Small Street to a house opposite Chequer Lane in Narrow Wine Street, where he makes and sells chocolate as usual'; and some time later, 'he has removed to Union Street, opposite the upper gate of St James's Market, where he keeps his shop for the sale of Churchman's Patent and other sorts of

chocolate nibs and cocoa.' At the premises in Union Street he erected a Watt's steam engine to work his machinery – the first in Bristol!

Van Houten's invention of the cocoa press, in 1828, at Weesp in Holland, meant that a much smoother chocolate drink could be produced. The world's first eating chocolate was manufactured in 1819 at Vevey, Switzerland, by François-Louis Cailler, who came up with a way of preparing and selling chocolate in individual blocks. Cailler did not market his chocolate as candy, however, and preferred to specialize in fondant making. Therefore, others would have it that the first solid eating chocolate was made in 1847 by Fry & Sons, who combined cocoa with sugar and cocoa butter to obtain a solid chocolate. It was a further twenty years before milk chocolate appeared, the creation of Daniel Peter in Switzerland

who added condensed milk, which had been developed by Henri Nestlé, to chocolate.

Many of these early chocolate-manufacturing companies had Quaker founders. Zephaniah Fry, Joseph's grandfather, was one of the younger and more devoted followers of George Fox. John Cadbury opened a tea and coffee business at 93 Bull Street, Birmingham, in 1824, and later went on to build his factory and garden village at Bournville on the out-skirts of the city. John Rowntree was descended from a Pickering farmer, who him-self went into grocery selling, but whose brother, Henry Isaac Rowntree, bought a small cocoa business in York in 1860 and developed the embryo of the huge company it is today.

One reason for this is that Quakers were encouraged to abstain from alcohol. Beer at this time was still England's main beverage – tea, coffee and chocolate being expensive. The new chocolate-making

Mars *ARE MARVELLOUS!*

You'll certainly agree! Just taste these chunks of sheer delicious goodness made with *chocolate* to sustain, *glucose* to energise, *milk* to nourish you. Ask your sweet shop for Mars.

MARS LTD., SLOUGH, BUCKS

Assorted SPANGLES

3ᵈ and only ONE POINT

ROWNTREE'S FRUIT GUMS

Bite the sparkle of a rippling stream!

Gay as the darts of sun on water, sweet as the song of a tinkling stream, merry as dancing, tumbling ripples—that's CRUNCHIE! Taste the luscious flavour of it—munch its crispy golden centre—CRUNCHIE munching is really something!

4ᴰ

CRUNCHIE

makes exciting biting!

companies saw and developed ways in which they could bring non-alcoholic beverages to the masses at affordable prices. They also set out to promote the idea that cocoa was an ideal addition to people's diets, containing as it does carbohydrates, albuminoids and mineral matter – a complete and perfect food. Interestingly, in the past chocolate was advertised as a weight-increasing product, and this was considered to be a virtue.

Terry's of York was founded by Joseph Terry, who was actually trained as an apothecary. He later formed a partnership with a Mr Bayldon and a Mr Berry, and their company imported citrus peel and made confectionery near Bootham Bar in York. By 1830 a series of new partners had come and gone, and Joseph Terry, apothecary, baker, confectioner and peel-importer, found himself on his own with a factory in Brearley Yard and a 'front shop' in St Helen's Square, near the Mansion House. However, his hard

NEW...far and away the best catch in chocolate treats

BOUNTY, WITH MILKIER, JUICIER COCONUT THAN EVEN SOUTH-SEA ISLANDERS EVER KNEW

BOUNTY, SMOTHERED THICK WITH FULL-CREAM MILK CHOCOLATE. TWO BIG CHUNKY BARS FOR 6ᵈ

ENJOY ONE TODAY!

"TRUMPETER-R-RR! WHY AREN'T YOU SOUNDING NOW?"

"I'M FINISHING MY MURRAYMINT"

work and resilience paid off, and soon he had a reputation for cakes and comfits, sugar sweet, candied peel, marmalade, mushroom ketchup and medicated lozenges. His list price for 1867 contained over 400 separate items, but only 13 of these were chocolate products. Soon Joseph Terry & Sons were displaying their products at national exhibitions, and in

1899 won the Gold Award for confectionery at the National Temperance Catering Exhibition. They produced their Britannia assortment prior to the First World War, Spartan in 1921 and All Gold in 1932.

Most popular brands of sweets and chocolate have been introduced over the last century or so. Rowntree's Fruit Pastilles appeared in 1881, their Fruit Gums in 1893, Black Magic in 1933, Kit Kat (then Chocolate Crisp) and Aero in 1935, Dairy Box in 1936, Smarties in 1937, Polo in 1948 and After Eight in 1962. Cadbury's Dairy Milk chocolate was introduced in 1905, Plain Tray in 1914, with Milk Tray a year later. Fry's Turkish Delight came in 1914 and Crunchie in 1929. Between 1929 and 1938 Cadbury's introduced no fewer than 189 new lines.

The Mars Bar, Snickers Bar, Maltesers and Milky Way are some of the bestselling confectionery brands. Frank C. Mars used a mixture of milk chocolate, corn syrup, sugar, milk, hydrogenated vegetable oil and other ingredients, including malt, butter and egg whites, to produce his chocolate bars. He launched Milky Way in 1923, to instant success, and the Snickers Bar seven years later. Maltesers were introduced in 1936, originally marketed as 'a portable malted drink in a box'. At the time

six flavours:
GOOSEBERRY
RASPBERRY
PEAR
LEMON
PINEAPPLE
TANGERINE
½ lb 2'4 1 lb 4'8

The only sweets with these lovely fruit liqueur centres
MELTIS LIMITED · BEDFORD · ENGLAND

malted drinks were popular, but expensive, and Maltesers soon became a favourite sweet, being convenient and relatively cheap.

The origin of Easter eggs stretches back many centuries. The use of eggs to celebrate important festivals dates from pre-Christian times — the Jews used eggs symbolically during Passover, and Pasche eggs were held by the Egyptians to be a sacred emblem of the 'renovation' of mankind after the Deluge. Later, in Tudor times, it is said that the Pope sent Henry VIII an Easter egg in a silver case. The chocolate Easter egg is a nineteenth-century creation, which came from Germany, although today the Germans tend to use the rabbit as an Easter

symbol. Our chocolate companies have made the most of the commercial potential for Easter eggs and just about every brand of chocolate and sweet has a corresponding egg and probably an advent calendar, too. Cadbury's are perhaps one of the best innovators in this market with their highly successful Creme Egg and their recent introduction of the Squegg – a square Easter egg.

Today, sweets and chocolates are regarded as a nice treat and, by most of us, as just a bit sinful. Despite their origins, they are now rarely associated with health-giving properties – rather the opposite – and while chewing sugar-free gum is cited by some dentists as being good for our teeth, we all know that most sweets lead to fillings. Also, having no shortage of more nutritious foods, we can hardly pretend that we need the energy or the weight-increasing calories. Still, sales of chocolates and sweets have never been higher, and it can still be argued, for those guilty chocolate lovers, that chocolate is good for you.

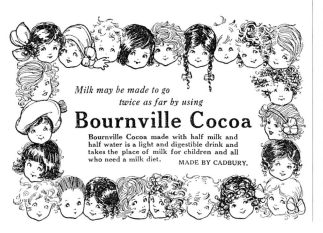

The Staff of Life
BREAD

Since ancient times bread has been a staple part of many people's diets, but its availability and quality has always depended on the success of the wheat harvest.

Christ instructed his disciples to break bread in remembrance of him and, ever since, the Christian Church has given special significance to bread. In religious terms, it has come to mean the essence of spiritual life. However, the Church has also recognized the physical need for everyday bread. In early British history it was customary that when the new grain was harvested a Loaf Mass would be held, and people celebrated with games, dancing and feasting. In early Victorian times the Harvest Festival was introduced into the Church calendar, and in many churches and chapels a loaf of bread, shaped like a sheaf of corn, was placed among the fruit, flowers and vegetables that made up the harvest display.

We do not know where the wheat plant originated, but it is likely that wheat was eaten as early as 10–15,000 years ago, probably being chewed straight from the husk, or mixed into a form of porridge, before people thought to grind and bake the light brown grains.

The Ancient Chinese, Greeks and Egyptians grew and harvested wheat and made bread. The ancient Egyptians were probably the first to make white bread, although the sifted flour was reserved for the ruling classes. They are also credited as being the first to make leavened bread.

In medieval times diseased grain is known to have sometimes led to severe poisoning, and in more modern times many city dwellers could only get very poor quality bread. Even in rural areas there was difficulty finding wholesome grain in June and July at the end of the harvest year.

For a long time, crops in Britain were very poor and wheat had to be brought in from abroad. It is recorded that in 1795, in Birmingham, wheat was damp and mouldy, the flour

BELOW LEFT (FACING PAGE) AND ABOVE: *Early attempts at bread making.*
RIGHT: *The old Warburtons bakery.*

on the grounds that it was injurious to them; however, the jury found that the objects of the company were laudable. Other cities also took steps to regulate matters. In Leeds, for example, the Leeds Flour Society was set up and other cities and towns had similar institutions.

In many British villages, but especially in rural parts of Yorkshire, oatcakes were a cheaper alternative to bread. In some places these were traditionally known as havercakes, from the Norse word *haverí*, meaning oat. The oatcake can either be made from a liquid batter or from a stiff dough that has been rolled out into thin cakes, and which is then cooked on a heated slab called a bakestone. Oatcakes are still popular today, especially as biscuits to be eaten with cheese.

Most of the bread we enjoy requires either yeast, a by-product of the brewing industry, or some other raising agent to be mixed in with

was sour, and the insides of the loaves were a loathsome mess – a grey sticky paste. In Victorian times poor people often ate bread made of rye, lentils and oatmeal, and housewives tried to make bread with only half the quantity of flour, making up the rest with potatoes or other vegetables. Some bakers were even said to add soap! All of these 'additives' certainly made for a heavy and very unappetizing loaf.

Due to these problems, a co-operative by the name of Union Mills was formed in Birmingham to supply people with good flour and good bread. Union Mills was hated by local millers and bakers and was even prosecuted the flour. Alfred Bird, a manufacturing chemist in Birmingham, noticed that soldiers fighting in the field of war suffered from a lack of proper bread. It was difficult to create a suitable mobile oven, and even more difficult to keep yeast active – yeast needs to be kept in specific conditions in order for it to rise, especially warm ones, and is easily killed off. So, in 1843, Alfred Bird invented a fermenting powder that could be used as a raising agent in the place of yeast. He sent one of his bread loaves, stamped with the Birmingham Corporation seal, to the head of the War Department, the Duke of Newcastle, and in return he received an order for a supply of his powder. Today we know this as baking powder. It was a big step forward in bread and cake making.

Alexander McDougall set himself up as a manufacturing chemist in 1845. Five of his sons joined the business and in 1864 the firm patented a substitute for yeast. The McDougall brothers were the first to use the term 'self-raising' flour and they revolutionized home baking. McDougall's first tried to interest bakers in bags of 'phosphatic yeast substitute', but as this did not prove popular, they purchased flour and mixed in the yeast substitute themselves. However, the flour was bought from several different millers and the standards of quality varied. To overcome the problem, the McDougalls became millers themselves. The business flourished and the McDougalls built their own mill in Manchester, and then, in 1869, another in Millwall, London; thus they were able to supply most of the country.

Gradually people started to take steps towards commercial bread production. In 1870 Thomas and Ellen Warburton took over a small grocery business on Blackburn Road, Bolton, but by the middle of the decade sales had slumped. Then Ellen came up with the idea of

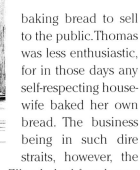

baking bread to sell to the public. Thomas was less enthusiastic, for in those days any self-respecting house-wife baked her own bread. The business being in such dire straits, however, the next day Ellen baked four loaves and six flour cakes. While they were still hot, she put them in the window and within the hour they were all sold! The next day she doubled her quantities and again they sold very quickly; within a week she was baking full time and even then she could not keep up with demand. The family soon turned their backs on the grocery business and renamed their shop 'Warburtons the Bakers'.

When Thomas's health deteriorated due to the long hours and heavy work, his nephew, Henry, a master baker, took over the business. Before long he moved the company to larger premises in the Diamond Jubilee bakery. At the turn of the century Warburtons started making deliveries in a horse-drawn van. Year by year the business grew, and in 1915 Henry's wife, Rachel, declared open the Model Bakery in front of a crowd of 500 people, including the mayor of Bolton. In 1930 Henry Warburton himself became Mayor of Bolton. He also became Chairman of Bolton Wanderers Football Club. They were good days for baking!

Today, with fifth-generation family members at the helm, and eight bakeries, Warburtons produces over a million loaves of bread every day and is the market leader in Lancashire, Yorkshire and the North East. It also exports many products overseas, particularly its Soreen Fruity Malt Loaf.

The need for improvements in the quality of most bread was something Richard Smith also picked up on. In the 1880s he conceived the idea of lightly cooking vitamin-rich wheatgerm in steam, so as to conserve its nourishing qualities and make it more healthy to eat. In 1886 he patented 'Smith's Patent Germ Flour', which was marketed by S. Fitton & Son Ltd, who were millers in Macclesfield. In 1890 the company ran a competition to find a new name for their increasingly popular bread. The winning suggestion was 'Hovis', which had been constructed from the Latin phrase *hominis vis* – 'the strength of man'. Hovis first appeared in the shops that year. For many years it was hand baked and produced in small bakeries; each loaf was cooked in tins, which were specially moulded so that the word 'HOVIS' would be imprinted on the sides of each loaf, promoting

ABOVE: *Each Hovis loaf was baked in a specially-moulded tin so that the word 'HOVIS' would be imprinted on the side.*

brand awareness. In 1957 Hovis merged with McDougalls to become Hovis-McDougall Ltd, and in 1961 Rank Hovis McDougall Ltd was the biggest group in the milling industry. In 1968 McDougall's were also responsible for bringing together a number of different bread-baking enterprises to form British Bakeries Ltd, which produces such well-known brands as Mother's Pride and Nimble.

Around the turn of the twentieth century people started to develop machinery to help with commercial bread making. In 1928 Otto Frederick Rohwedder, a retired Missouri jeweller, made the first commercial bread slicer. It took a while to catch on, but by 1930 Continental Baking were using his machine. They launched a sliced and wrapped loaf called Wonder Bread, along with claims that it would give people 'strong bodies'. By 1933 80 per cent of all bread sold commercially in the United States was pre-sliced, and by World War II the expression 'the next best thing to sliced bread' had entered the common parlance, meaning anything new and desirable.

Thomas Allinson was born at Grange-over-Sands, on the edge of the Lake District, in 1858. He later went to Edinburgh University where he studied medicine, and he became a doctor

AT THE TIME OF THE
JUBILEE OF GEORGE THE THIRD
The Price of Bread was 1s. 1¼d., now what a change, this year of the
JUBILEE OF QUEEN VICTORIA!
R. J. GRUBB has much pleasure in stating that this day at his establishments the
Price of Bread has been Reduced.
BEST BREAD 4½ d.
....
Household Bread 4d.
3 Loaves for 1s.

Finest Pastry Flour, 11d. per bag of 7 lbs.
Good ditto, 9d. per bag of 7 lbs.
Best Hungarian Flour, 10d. per bag of 5 lbs.
Splendid Scotch Oatmeal, 2d. per lb., 2|3 per Stone.
Groatine 8d. per 3 lb. packet.

Best Establishment in Oxford for Poultry and Horse Food, &c.

Barley, Maize, Wheat, Buckwheat, &c., exceedingly low.
CRUSHED CORN FOR HORSES, 6s. per Cwt.
This Corn is unequalled in Oxford or elsewhere.
OATS from 9s. per sack. CHAFF, 4s. 6d. per Cwt.
BARLEY MEAL, 9s. per Sack, 4 Sacks for 34s.

OBSERVE:—22 Queen Street. | 16, St. Clement's.
Castle Mills. | 15, St. Aldate's.

September 7th, 1887.

ALDEN & CO., PRINTERS, OXFORD.

flourmill in the world. Dr Tom Allinson's standards are still upheld in the famous wrapped bread that Allied Bakeries produce – 'wi nowt

when he was only 23. He was keenly interested in how diet affected people's health and was already an advocate of wholemeal bread. He later wrote two books: *A System of Hygenic Medicine* and *The Advantages of Wholemeal Bread.* He set up his own medicinal practice in London, and a few years later acquired Cyclone Mills in Bethnal Green. He formed the Natural Food Company, coining the phrase 'Health without Medicine'.

He sold his flour to bakers and provided them with certificates that stated that they were making wholemeal bread to his standard and with his flour. If patients did not have a bakery nearby, he encouraged them to bake their own bread using his flour. In 1921 the company acquired Queens Mill in Castleford and it is now the largest stone-grinding

round-the-clock sessions at the gaming boards. To prevent him from having to break from his gambling, the Earl got his servant to bring him pieces of meat between two slices of bread whenever he was peckish. This instant meal soon caught on – and the Earl's name with it. Captain James Cook honoured the Earl by naming a group of islands in the Pacific Ocean 'The Sandwich Islands', although today we know them as the Hawaiian Islands.

Today our sandwiches are rather more refined. Many of us enjoy a filled baguette – a long thin loaf whose name translates as 'little rod', or a sandwich made with Italian ciabatta bread – ciabatta meaning 'slipper'. Bagels were originally an American–Jewish creation, taking their name from the Yiddish word *beigen*. Americans sometimes refer to them as 'the donut with the Jewish education'. Made from unsalted yeast dough, which is simmered in water and then baked, these chewy bread rings – whether plain, seeded, onion or cinnamon flavour – are becoming increasingly popular in Britain.

taken out'. Allied Bakeries was founded in 1935 by Garfield Weston, and now produces such well-known brands as Kingsmill, Sunblest, Mighty White and HiBran.

Some breads were made in consequence of a particular event or for an individual's preference. In 1683 the Austrians stopped the Ottoman Turks from occupying Vienna. To commemorate the victory Viennese bakers created the croissant, which is shaped like the crescent in the Turkish flag.

The sandwich is attributed to the English nobleman, Jemmy Twitcher, fourth Earl of Sandwich and notorious gambler in the Court of George III; the Earl was famous for his

The Melba Toast takes its name from Dame Nellie Melba, the famous opera singer. The story goes that Nellie loved to visit Delmonico's, her favourite New York restaurant, where she

adored the chef's specialities. However, on one occasion she was slimming, and, on learning this, the chef presented her with pâté on a very thinly-sliced piece of toasted bread. Nellie was delighted, and the chef named his creation in her honour – or literally as a 'toast' to her. Today Melba Toast is made and distributed throughout Europe by Van der Meulen-Hallum BV of Holland.

Across its counties, Britain has many different types of traditional, unbranded breads, which many people still prefer to buy. Many of them are known by their distinctive shape. The crusty cottage loaf is a much-loved loaf, generally made of two pieces of dough, one on top of the other. Another favourite is the tin or long tin loaf, simply named after the tin in which the loaves are baked. Cobs and Coburgs are round loaves, the Coburg being marked out by two short cuts across the top set at right angles to each other. In Yorkshire, flat bread cakes are often referred to as oven bottoms, and in the very northern parts of Yorkshire, starting around Middleham, a local flat, round, plain bread loaf, rather similar to an oven bottom, is known as a Stottie.

Yorkshire certainly has its fair share of local breads. Traditionally, spice bread would be made in May to be served at a communal tea, whilst at Christmas time a rich fruity Yule bread was baked, which was then sliced and buttered. Less seasonal were fatty cakes, which as their name suggests, were made with flour, butter, dripping or lard, and sad cakes, which are made with flour, baking powder, lard and milk. Yorkshire is not unique, however. Every region has its own many specialities, from the Welsh Bara Brith, a loaf embellished by dried fruit that has been soaked overnight in hot tea, to the bannock, a dome-shaped fruit loaf unique to Scotland.

Today we can still enjoy almost all of these breads, as well as fruity teacakes and buns, savoury baps and a wide selection of rolls. And with choices such as sun-dried tomato bread, sunflower-seed, and muesli bread, lunch and teatime have never been more exciting.

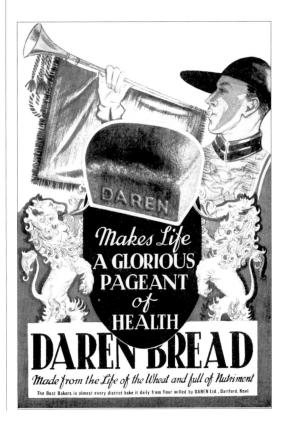

A Jam-Packed Market
FRUIT PRESERVES

Preserving fruit began on a small, home-cooking basis as housewives discovered that fruit could be preserved when cooked with sugar.

In the nineteenth century, commercially-produced fruit preserve was an aristocratic dish, and to call it 'jam' was considered to be the height of vulgarity.

At this time, most commercial jam makers were based in London, but this made things difficult for fruit farmers living in such places as Essex or Cambridgeshire. Getting their freshly-picked fruit to its destination in good condition was not an easy feat, and therefore many fruit farmers started preserving their fruit on their own farms. The Chivers and the Wilkins were two such families.

The Chivers family, along with thousands of their Huguenot brothers, had fled from their native France to England following Louis XIV's Revocation of the Edict of Nantes, which meant that they could no longer worship freely as Protestants. John Chivers was born about 1787 and, along with his brother William, worked hard on their land in Histon, near Cambridge, growing both corn and fruit. In the early 1830s they were joined by John's three sons, Philip, Stephen and Thomas. They sent their fruit to London markets, but this was a two-day wagon trip of over a hundred miles. Usually three

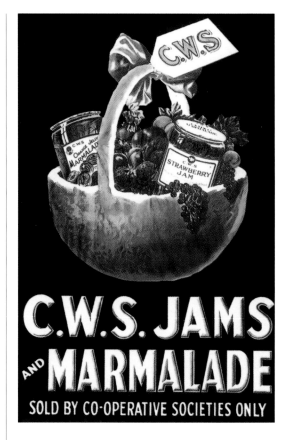

C.W.S. JAMS
ᴬᴺᴰ MARMALADE
SOLD BY CO-OPERATIVE SOCIETIES ONLY

wagons were sent, two carrying fruit and the third carrying wood faggots to lay over the worst parts of the road.

By the late 1860s Stephen Chivers had had enough and decided they should have their own depot. He soon sent his own sons, William and John, aged 18 and 13 respectively, to manage a wholesale depot in Bradford. There the boys discovered that their best customers were local jam makers. In 1873 Stephen Chivers & Sons started making jam at Histon, selling it in jars, which held 2, 4 or 6 lbs, and later also in decorated jugs. The jam was

poured into warmed jars using silver-plated ladles and parchment covers were tied on. Handwritten labels were then fixed to the jars – in fact they were written by hand until 1905!

Demand grew and in 1874 the company purchased an orchard adjoining Histon station. There they built a four-storey building to house a steam boiling plant and other up-to-date equipment. This was originally called Victoria Works, although in 1910 it was renamed the Orchard Factory. By the 1890s posters advertising Chivers jams and jellies were common in cities throughout England, and pictures of their farms and products were

Inviting you to BREAKFAST

...with
The Aristocrat
of the
Breakfast Table

CHIVERS
Olde English
MARMALADE

even displayed by the London Underground. By 1914 Chivers owned 4,000 acres and this had doubled by 1934.

Jam production is seasonal, but Chivers realized they needed to retain good staff by being able to employ them throughout the year. To achieve this they started making Seville Orange Marmalade in 1885 and, in subsequent years, table jellies, custard powder, lemon curd, Christmas puddings, mincemeat and other such products. In 1907 they introduced Olde English Marmalade, known as the 'Aristocrat of the Breakfast Table', and by 1911 the company had received its first royal warrant. Today, in addition to Chivers goods, Hartley, Moorhouse and Rose's products are manufactured at Histon.

South-east of Histon is the village of Tiptree, in Essex, where Arthur Charles Wilkin was born in 1835. Initially he went to work as an office boy in London, but sorely missed the green fields and open air of his birthplace. At the age of 24 he took over the family farm and started growing fruit. He became one of a group of growers who supplied Mr Blackwell, then senior partner in the firm of Crosse and Blackwell. Arthur also supplied some London jam makers, but found this fraught with problems. When the railway company he used put his fruit in coal trucks and then covered them with tarpaulin, things went from bad to worse.

In about 1883 matters came to a head. Arthur Wilkin was now 48 years old and had a wife and five children to support. However, he had heard that Mr Gladstone, the Prime Minister, had made a speech encouraging tenant farmers to grow fruit and make jam. Whilst in some agricultural circles this had caused ridicule, Arthur and two of his friends were inspired by the notion, seeing it as an opportunity. They employed a first-rate London jam maker to guide their enterprise and he set up a deal with an Australian merchant, who agreed to take all the whole-fruit jam they could make. The merchant insisted that the jam

Harvest Time in CHIVERS' ORCHARDS

" Some folk seem to think that fruit just grows. Well it does and it doesn't. To get Plums, Strawberries or Raspberries like ours means hard work all the year round and you've got to know your job. Our factory people over the road know theirs too — for they certainly seem to make Chivers Jam the way most people like it, even though it now has to fit in with war-time standards." Farmers are short of hands this year for harvesting, so if there are farms or orchards near, do offer *YOUR* help *NOW*.

Sorry, no more Chivers Jellies until Victory is won but

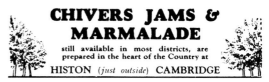

CHIVERS JAMS &
MARMALADE
still available in most districts, are
prepared in the heart of the Country at
HISTON *(just outside)* CAMBRIDGE

In such a countryside grew the fruits for this REAL JAM

should not contain glucose, colouring matter or preservatives, and that it should be called 'conserve' to distinguish it from poorer products. He also wanted the labels to read 'made by the Britannia Preserving Company' – 'Britannia' being a good trading name for Australia at the time.

The first batch of jam was made in Mrs Wilkin's kitchen, using her own recipes. Later Arthur acquired three boiling pans, which he set up in a barn, and hired two traction engines to provide the power to heat them. Soon he and his friends were in business, and Arthur

Hold on to Hartley's! This delicious real fruit jam has not altered in quality by one single berry, or by one ounce of the pure white sugar which has always gone into Hartley's jam-making. See those good deep orchard tones through the glass of the pots. That is your guarantee that Hartley's are still offering you the same goodness and real-fruit nourishment for your money.

A PROMISE

PEACE may be quick or slow in coming, but you will always be able to rely on the name 'HARTLEY'S' for Fresh Fruit Jams at the lowest price at which jam as good as Hartley's can possibly be sold, that they will keep their word UP and PRICES DOWN as long as is humanly possible. That is our determined policy.

HARTLEY'S
The greatest name in jam-making

NO PULP NO PRESERVATIVES!

No Glucose or colouring matter is ever used in Hartley's Jams and Marmalade.
Only Delicious Fresh-picked Fruit and Purest White Sugar – the kind you use at Home.
That's how we get the real Home-Made Flavour and why Hartley's is always Best Value for Money.
Make sure it's

Hartley's
JAMS & MARMALADE

was able to send Mr Gladstone a box of strawberry jam to thank him for the idea – in return he received a letter offering further encouragement.

Things were often far from easy, however. Sometimes the pans had to be kept boiling all night to cope with the crop and Wilkin nearly gave up as bad debts mounted and expenses became almost unbearable. Still, they struggled on, expanding the Wilkin's range of products to include marmalades, pickles, sauces and vinegars. In 1905 the company adopted the trademark 'Tiptree' and commenced trading as Wilkin & Sons Ltd. At this period, at any one time, up to a thousand men, women and children would be involved in picking fruit. In 1911 Wilkin & Sons Ltd received its first royal warrant from King George V. Today the company is still independent, with Arthur's great-grandson Peter Wilkin as chairman. The company prides itself on its high-quality products, which are still made in small batches, and such is the demand from London hotels that two lorries are used to

make daily deliveries. Today its products are exported to more than sixty countries.

Twenty-four-year-old Fred Duerr was a commercial traveller who, after his marriage to 16-year-old Mary Naylor, went to live in Heywood, near Rochdale in Lancashire. He later became a grocery commission agent and in 1881 met the buyer for the Heywood Co-operative Society, Honest John Butterworth, who told him that he could not get high-quality preserves that were free from additives. Honest John then asked Fred if his wife, whose jam-making skills were legendary in the area, would consider making jams for the Society, saying that if she agreed he would take all she could make.

Soon the jam making was in hand and Fred took the jars to the store on a handcart. In 1884 Fred built their first factory at Guide Bridge, between Manchester and Ashton, it being the most modern of its kind in Britain. Fred Duerr

chose all the fruit himself and claimed that he had a secret method of preserving it so that it could be stored for use during the winter. As far back as 1905 Duerr's pioneered vacuum-sealing jars, which enabled the jam to be kept indefinitely.

The founder had worked hard for his success, but he also ensured that his staff were well looked after, and they received good wages and half-yearly bonuses. Duerr's is still a family business – fourth-generation Tony Duerr OBE is now chairman and his sons are also involved in the business. In 1995 they opened a new complex at Wythenshawe and are now the largest independent producer in the jam and preserves market. In addition to their jams, the company now produces 250,000 jars of peanut butter each day, and has made a hundred million jars of jam since Mary first went to work in her kitchen.

Cassell's Household Guide of about 1870 suggests that rhubarb jam, mixed with orange marmalade, is an excellent tonic relish for delicate appetites. Marmalade is said to come from the name of an Indian fruit, not unlike an orange, called *Aegle marmelos*, or Indian Bael, from which a conserve was made. In Greece it was once called *melimelon*, sweet apple, and the Romans called it *melimelum*. It came to England by way of Portugal, where it was known as *marmelada*, meaning quince conserve – from which fruit it was once made. Another popular story, though it is likely to be apocryphal, is that when Mary Queen of Scots was out of sorts, the only food that could tempt her was a conserve of oranges – hence the name 'Marie *malade*', sick Mary, which in time became marmalade. Today, marmalade is made mainly from oranges, generally including some of the peel.

The town most famous for its marmalade is Dundee, in Scotland. In Victorian times Keiller were making over 1,000 tons a year, which filled 1.5 million jars. They used 3,000 chests of the finest bitter oranges, which were imported from Seville in Spain. Production was seasonal – being generally from the beginning of December until the end of March.

James Robertson started work as a thread-mill worker in Paisley, but seeing little future there became an apprentice to a local grocer. Eventually he opened his own store, and there, in 1864, he was persuaded by a salesman to purchase a barrel of bitter oranges. They didn't sell and Robertson was anxious that he had wasted precious funds. Robertson's wife, Marion, suggested making them into marmalade. The jars soon sold and the Robertsons realized they were on to a good thing. Two years later Marion could no longer cope in her small kitchen and they decided to

move their marmalade production to a proper factory. Marion is credited with coining the name Golden Shred for her unique, clear marmalade; the lemon-flavoured Silver Shred was introduced some time later.

Today, one of the things Robertson's is most associated with is its famous golly. When a Robertson's director was visiting the United States, just before the First World War, he came across golliwogs for the first time and decided that they would be an appealing motif to use on the Robertson's jars. Soon afterwards the design was incorporated into each of their product labels. The first enamel golly brooches and badges were made as part of a promotion in 1930, starting with Golly Golfer. Since then, although the golly has at times been criticized for not being politically correct, over fifteen million have been given away. They are now

collectors' items and the golly has a number of fan clubs.

Few housewives have time to make their own jam today, and there is now a vast range of jams and preserves in our shops for us to purchase ready-made. Interestingly, most of us still want that homemade look and taste, and to believe that a good percentage of fruit has gone into our jams. Perhaps like Arthur Wilkin, we too like the idea of ripe orchards and the freshness of the countryside.

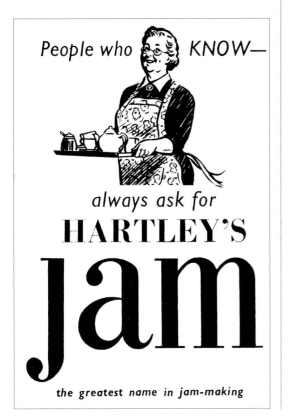

A Nice Cup of . . .
BEVERAGES & SOFT DRINKS

Most British people could not imagine life without the traditional cuppa, which has come to be something of a national beverage. Likewise, many cannot face the day until they have had a mug of coffee, and young people throughout the world may not be able to picture a time when cans of Coca-Cola and other bottled and cartoned drinks were not readily available for consumption. In fact, although 'artificial mineral waters' were being sold commercially in the late 1700s, soft drinks were only widely marketed in the twentieth century. And while tea and coffee were known and cultivated in ancient civilizations, they have only been drunk by most British people since the mid-1800s, ale being the common beverage until this time.

The word 'coffee' comes from Caffa, a town in Ethiopia, where the fruit of the *Coffea arabica*, coffee tree, was chewed as a stimulant. The plant produces green berries, which, when mature, turn dark red. Inside these are two pods containing the coffee beans, which are roasted and ground or crushed, and mixed with milk or water to form the dark liquid infusion we are familiar with today.

It is said the Arabian philosopher and physician Avicenna first invented coffee in about AD 1000. He called the drink *bunc* and believed it to have medicinal value. It was not until about the sixteenth century, however, that coffee became an accepted social beverage in Arabia and Persia. Coffee first arrived in Europe in the seventeenth century – from Arabia, the Far East and Jamaica. The first coffee house opened in Oxford, and we know that when a Greek man by the name of Canopios visited the city, in 1637, he drank coffee in preference to ale. Coffee became an important item of commerce and coffee houses opened, which not only became popular but

LEFT: *An early London coffee house* c.*1705.*

began to rival ale houses. By 1700 there were 2,500 coffee houses in London, including Lloyd's Coffee House, in Lombard Street, where the big insurance company was born, initially as shipping insurers.

During 1879, the *Illustrated London News* reported the several occasions on which members of parliament were present at the openings of coffee houses, and coffee certainly found favour with Mr Gladstone who made a speech in praise of the drink and its importance in preventing intemperance. Drunkenness was a widespread problem at the time, particularly amongst the working classes, as gin and ale were cheap. When The Lucky Dog Tavern, which specialized in coffee, was opened in Clare Market, very near to Drury Lane in central London, the *Illustrated London*

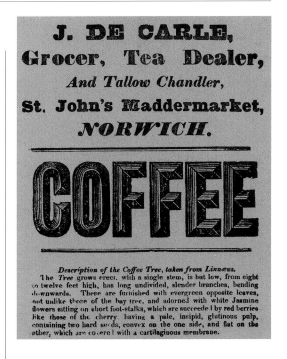

J. DE CARLE,
Grocer, Tea Dealer,
And Tallow Chandler,
St. John's Maddermarket,
NORWICH.

COFFEE

Description of the Coffee Tree, taken from Linnæus.
The *Tree* grows erect, with a single stem, is but low, from eight to twelve feet high, has long undivided, slender branches, bending downwards. These are furnished with evergreen opposite leaves, not unlike those of the bay tree, and adorned with white Jasmine flowers sitting on short foot-stalks, which are succeeded by red berries like those of the cherry, having a pale, insipid, glutinous pulp, containing two hard seeds, convex on the one side, and flat on the other, which are covered with a cartilaginous membrane.

News reported that it was 'desired to provide food and drink, thoroughly wholesome and well prepared, at a moderate cost, in order to meet the wants of a large population which now throngs the public houses in the neighbourhood. There is probably no district in London where more sin and distress are continually caused by intemperance.'

However, coffee houses themselves were not always respectable establishments. In 1657, James Furr, who kept The Rainbow at Lower Temple Gate, was prosecuted for creating a nuisance by making and vending a liquor called coffee. No self-respecting lady would be seen in a coffee house and by the early eighteenth century many were of such ill repute that they were closed down.

As it was, many people probably never got to taste a 'real' cup of coffee, for

have been created at the request of the Gordon Highlanders, who wanted a coffee drink that could be easily brewed when the army was away on field campaigns. It was certainly an instant success with the army, and sales at home and abroad soared – reaching as far afield, in the early twentieth century, as Russia, Australia, the Americas and even tropical islands. The original label featured an officer of the Gordon Highlanders with his Sikh bearer holding a tray with a coffee pot and cups, and carried the slogan, 'Ready, Aye Ready'.

In 1889, it was put about by the Press that the consumption of coffee was falling off due to people's preference for cocoa. One who had more faith in the market for coffee was Kentucky-born Joel Cheek, then a 21-year-old travelling salesman for a firm of wholesale grocers. Coffee proved a fascination to him and he spent many hours selecting various beans and roasting them for different periods,

owing to its high price and the cheap tricks of those that sold it, it was often adulterated with chicory or worse. It is interesting to note that as early as 1892 penny-in-the-slot machines had been installed in Paris for the sale of drinks such as Malaga wine and hot coffee. *Chambers's Journal* looked forward to the day they would be available in Britain, providing that the coffee served 'should be fit to drink, which it very frequently is not'.

One of the first coffee brands, and possibly the first instant coffee, was Camp Coffee, which is made from a coffee essence mixed with chicory and sugar. However, others claim Nescafé was the first instant coffee, being introduced in Switzerland by Nestlé in 1938. Camp Coffee was the invention of R. Paterson & Sons, a Glasgow company, in 1885, and is said to

China, the land of flowers and legends, is also the land of tea, and many stories have been passed down about its origin. One is of how, in AD510, the Indian Prince Bodhidharma, a pious monk and missionary, landed on the coast of China. Wanting to set an example of piety, he vowed he would not sleep until his mission was accomplished. For many years he was wakeful. He taught, prayed and meditated, but eventually was overcome by sleep. He was so disappointed by the weakness of his flesh that he cut off his eyelids and threw them to the ground. However, Buddha caused them to root and the first tea plant grew. The plant, with its leaves shaped like eyelids and its sleep-delaying properties, became the symbol of eternal wakefulness. Another legend tells how a Buddhist hermit was putting some wood from a dried tea plant on to a fire when some of the leaves fell into the pot in which he was boiling water for his evening meal – thus the first pot of tea.

creating new blends. By 1892 he felt he had found his 'perfect coffee blend', and that it was time to share it with the world. He managed to persuade the management of the Maxwell House luxury hotel in Nashville, Tennessee, to demonstrate his new blend, which was in itself quite a feat, for it was there that the President, senators, diplomats and leading Europeans stayed. Within weeks, distinguished guests were praising the new coffee and one of the first commercial blends had begun. President Theodore Roosevelt said of the coffee: 'Will I have another? Delighted! It's good to the last drop!' Very few of us have heard of Joel Cheek, and unfortunately the Maxwell House hotel was destroyed in a fire in 1961, but Maxwell House coffee is known throughout the world and is still very much a leading brand.

Today, there is a wide range of packaged coffee, which includes many instant brands. There is also a vast choice of over-the-counter coffee drinks – from double espresso through latte, to cappuccino. The word *cappuccino* actually means 'monk's hood' – the Italians associating the drink's peaked frothy top with this garment.

Tea has had a large impact on many civilizations – the Japanese have their tea cere-

BELOW: *The Maxwell House hotel which was destroyed by fire in 1961.*

monies, a sign of gracious living; in America in 1773 it was the British attempt to put a tax on tea that led to the 'Boston Tea Party', and eventually to the American War of Independence; and tea was behind the disgraceful Opium Wars between Britain and China.

Tea first came to Britain from China during Cromwell's time. It was marketed as a medicinal draught, being advertised in a London gazette as 'That excellent and by all physicians approved China drink'. In 1660, Samuel Pepys recorded in his diary, 'I did send for a cupp of tee (a China drink) of which I had never drunk before'. However, the drink didn't catch on until 1662, when Charles II's Portuguese wife brought a large chest of tea as part of her dowry. Suddenly tea became all the rage at court and everyone who was anyone rushed to purchase some – if they could. For tea was extortionate in price and the government soon taxed it heavily.

Not everyone was so delighted with tea, however, and it was put about that it was a drink only fit for women. Nor were people entirely sure how to drink it. It was some time before it was realized that boiling water made the best brew, and legend has it that when the widow of the Duke of Monmouth sent some tea to her friends in Scotland, they warmed it up, discarded the liquid, and ate the leaves as a vegetable.

Tea was originally taken green, without milk or sugar, at breakfast and after dinner. A huge snobbishness surrounded the drink. The blending and pouring of tea became an art, and it was important for all young ladies to know how to pour. There was also rivalry over the possession of tea sets; again only the finest families being able to afford the blue and white Chinese porcelain. Today, Norwich Castle Museum has a large collection of teapots, including the oldest known tea kettle. Early teacups had no handle, being held by the brim and base to avoid burning the fingers; it was this that led to holding the cup with the little finger sticking out.

It is said that Anna, Duchess of Bedford, started the idea of afternoon tea in 1840. Each afternoon she suffered a 'sinking feeling', which she found was relieved by a little light refreshment, tea and cakes. Her friends copied the idea and the British custom of afternoon tea was born. Ladies did not go to tea and coffee houses but public tea gardens were popular. London's first real tea shop opened in 1884, followed by others such as J. Lyons' Corner Houses, and the fashion for going out to tea has continued through the elegance of Edwardian tea-rooms and tea dances to today's afternoon outings for cream tea.

Tea drinking was slow to infiltrate the general population, however, due to tea's high price, and for many years it was too expensive even for the middle classes. So scarce and valuable was tea, that only the mistress of the house would have keys to the tea caddy, and the leaves

would be used two or more times. It took an average ship between 12 and 15 months to sail

from China, and at first only British ships could enter British ports. Later, when this rule was changed, in 1849, the famous tea clippers were built to speed up the journey time and to beat foreign ships to harbour.

Thomas Twining acquired the now famous Tom's Coffee House in the Strand, London, in 1706, but as a sideline Twinings also sold loose tea and was the only coffee house ladies could buy tea from. Over seventy years later his grandson Richard, who was chairman of the Dealers of Tea, successfully persuaded William Pitt the Younger, Prime Minister at the time, to reduce the high tax on tea, which had already led to a flourishing black market, smuggling and to the American revolt. The resultant reduction in the price of tea was a major

influence in making it the popular drink it is today. In 1837 Twinings were granted their first royal warrant as 'Purveyor of Tea in Ordinary to Her Majesty', and the company has held royal warrants ever since. Twinings remains the oldest tea company, and the only one trading on the same site (interestingly, the Great Fire of London stopped just short of it), with the same name and the same product for nearly 300 years.

As tea drinking became more widespread, others discovered its market potential. In 1852,

William Sumner & Sons were listed as tea and coffee dealers, operating at the top of the Bull Ring in Birmingham. By the turn of the century William's son, John, and his grandson, also John, had a flourishing business with six travellers and quite a range of horse-drawn transport. Mary, young John's sister, had long suffered from indigestion. One day someone sent her a packet of tea with very small particles and this gave her great relief from her troubles. Mary encouraged her brother to sell the tea and he purchased thirty chests and packeted it. He then had to decide on a brand name. He eventually came up with 'Ty-Phoo Tips', which he felt had an oriental sound, was alliterative – hence memorable – and, while the word 'tips' could not be registered, 'Ty-Phoo' could be. It duly was – the double 'p' in 'Tipps' was a printer's error on the packaging.

In 1826, Honest John Horniman started to measure tea leaves in sealed paper packets with a guaranteed weight. His idea, and Horniman's Tea, had caught on. The first cardboard packets of Ty-Phoo Tips were hand-filled by girls using scoops, who then weighed them, before gluing and sealing them.

During the Second World War, the Ty-Phoo works was destroyed by bombs, but a special 'emergency blend' was introduced. It was packed by Brooke Bond Ltd and Lyons Ltd – a gesture much appreciated by Ty-Phoo.

In the early nineteenth century orphaned teenage brothers Joseph and Edward Tetley peddled salt from the back of a packhorse on the Yorkshire Moors. Later they added tea to their supplies, taking it to remote villages, which proved such a success that they set up as tea merchants. In about 1856 Joseph Tetley, with partner Joseph Ackland, formed Joseph Tetley & Co, Wholesale Tea Dealers. The company became involved with blending and packing, and the business extended to the United States. The American links became very important and through them Tetley saw continued success. One of their representatives brought back the concept of the teabag in 1939, although Tetley did not introduce teabags to the public until 1953. The Tea Council records show that the teabag was accepted in the United States as early as 1920, where it had originally been introduced so that customers could take away samples of new blends. There is also a claim that the Mazawattee Tea Company was in fact the first to introduce the teabag to Britain, the company installing a teabag-making machine imported from the

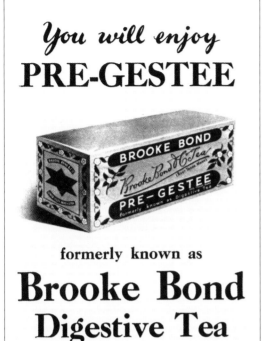

You will enjoy
PRE-GESTEE

formerly known as

Brooke Bond
Digestive Tea

Always <u>refreshes</u>,
always <u>revives</u>–
your cup of
P.G. Tips

CHANGE TO BROOKE BOND P.G. TIPS—*the tea you can really taste*

United States in 1948. When that company closed down, in 1952, the machine was transferred to the Aldgate factory of Brooke Bond.

Arthur Brooke was born in 1845 at Ashton-under-Lyne. His father had built up a good business as a wholesale tea merchant, but decided that young Arthur should enter the cotton trade. However, Arthur later returned to the declining family business, before starting his own firm in 1869. He opened for trade at 29 Market Street, Manchester, putting up a sign that read 'Brooke, Bond and Company'. There was no Mr Bond; he just felt the name sounded good. He only sold tea, coffee and sugar – and always on a cash-only basis, something which was unusual at this time but no doubt wise, many companies being crippled by credit and bad debt. Arthur regarded tea blending as a work of art. He would choose exact proportions from quality teas, mixing together those of the selected taste, colour or season. He wrote 'Brooke, Bond & Co' in his own flowing

of the Earl's envoys had saved the mandarin's life. Today Earl Grey is made from large-leafed China tea and bergamot oil and is but one of the many speciality teas the company produces.

In 1888 the price of tea fell, as Ceylon and India were providing China with competition in the market place. Tea was not grown in India until about 1840 when the Assam Tea Company was formed, and in Ceylon (now Sri Lanka) until the 1870s. However, their exports of tea grew dramatically. Between 1866 and 1886 exports of China tea doubled, but those from India increased fourteenfold. Indian tea was also favoured because this black tea was stronger and better prepared than China tea.

Thomas Lipton started his working life as a cabin boy. When he returned to his home town, Glasgow, he worked in his parents' shop and realized he could sell tea cheaply if he could produce it himself. In 1888 he bought several estates in Ceylon and soon began selling tea more cheaply than other retailers.

Tea was not easy pickings for everyone, however, especially those who had literally to do the picking. In 1880 *Chambers's Journal* reported on the dangers that tea planters faced in Assam where the climate was bad, with incessant rain. Many British workers died. The tea plant, *Camel-*

script on every packet and used it as his trademark. His staff proudly boasted that orders received in the 8 o'clock post were dispatched on the 9 o'clock trains!

The Co-operative Society had started giving 'dividend' stamps; Brooke Bond followed with Dividend Tea in 1935, each quarter-pound packet bearing a stamp worth 1d. Sixty stamps filled a card and this could be redeemed for five shillings. This was also the decade when Pre-Gestee was introduced, later becoming much better known as PG Tips. When commercial television arrived, Brooke Bond was an early advertiser, introducing the famous chimpanzees to the British public during Christmas 1956.

The Jackson family of Piccadilly fame has trading links in London going back to 1685. When the various businesses merged in the early nineteenth century they became Robert Jackson & Co. In 1830 the secret of the original Earl Grey tea blend was passed to one of the partners, having been entrusted to the 2nd Earl Grey by a celebrated Chinese mandarin – one

If you told Horlicks drinkers we hadn't changed Horlicks for 68 years, they'd just say

goodness

Horlicks have been making Horlicks since 1900. Sleep hasn't changed much in those 68 years. Neither has Horlicks.

Our experience has shown us that we found the original, best way to replenishing rest a long time ago. 68 years ago. The reason is simple. Horlicks is a very natural drink. Just the good things in life. For a good night's sleep. Nothing fancy. Nothing artificial. Comforting. Creamy. Good.

The food drink of the night

lia sinensis, is an evergreen shrub that grows to a height of about 4 feet, and is generally about three or four years old before the leaves are picked. Young leaves are picked from the bushes about every fortnight throughout the year, although in the mountainous regions such as the Himalayas growth stops during the winter months. In Darjeeling the tea plants are again situated at high altitudes, and again have to survive in an area of heavy rainfall, low temperatures and even occasional droughts.

Certain beverages have been developed to prevent 'Night Starvation' – and this was the claim of Horlicks during the early 1930s. The firm of J. & W. Horlick was formed in Chicago in 1873 by two English brothers, William and James Horlick. James was a qualified pharmacist and was interested in the work of Gail Borden, who, a few years earlier, had taken out a patent for the evaporation of condensed milk. James himself had experimented with the evaporation of a malt food and William had already started to manufacture an artificial infant food. In 1883 they registered the patent for 'malted milk' – an extract from a mash of malted barley and wheat flour mixed with fresh whole milk, this being evaporated to dryness under vacuum. The resultant powder could then be mixed with hot water to give a beverage suitable for invalids and infants. It was a success.

In the early 1890s James returned to England and opened an office in London, the factory at Slough being built between 1906–8. James's first London order was to supply Fortnum & Mason, the well-known grocers of Piccadilly. Arctic explorers Amundsen, Evans, Scott and Shackleton all took Horlicks Malted Milk with them on their arduous journeys. The words 'malted milk' were dropped during the early 1930s. However, it was still felt that a drink of Horlicks before bedtime maintained sugar levels, giving restful sleep.

Dr George Wander was a Swiss chemist who set up a laboratory in Berne in 1865. He was also interested in the nutritional values

of pure apple juice and containing no added sugar. It was also clear and sparkling, and free from sediment and metallic contact, being particularly good for the kidneys. In the same issue of that magazine, Stower's lemonade powder is advertised – a 4½d packet 'making 36 glasses of the most healthy and refreshing beverage on earth'. Stower's lime juice cordial is also mentioned in the *Windsor Journal* that year, being 'of delicious flavour, great strength, and absolutely pure. It is specially selected to be *Supplied to her Majesty the Queen*, which is the best possible proof of its superiority'. The *Windsor Journal* also carries an advertisement for Eiffel Tower lemonade, claiming that one of its advantages is that it is 'partly manufactured in Italy, in the midst of the lemon orchards'.

However, Jacob Schweppe, who was born at Witzenhausen in Germany in 1740, was manu-

of malt extract, and in 1904 he introduced Ovaltine. Doctors recognized its nutritional value and it quickly became a success in Switzerland. A British company was formed in 1909. At first, supplies were shipped in in bulk, but a small factory was opened at Kings Langley where the present buildings were put up in the 1920s. A 400-acre farm, supplying the company with its own milk and eggs, was established in 1929. In 1935 the Ovaltiney Club, which was sponsored by Ovaltine, was launched on Radio Luxembourg – the Club's song 'We are the Ovaltineys' becoming one of the more memorable advertising jingles.

Fruit squashes, packaged juices and fizzy drinks were not widely introduced to our markets until the twentieth century and households would make their own soft drinks including nettle beer, ginger beer, lemonade, elderflower cordial and rose-hip syrup.

In 1899, the *Strand Magazine* carried an advertisement for bottles of Pomril. The drink was described as light and non-alcoholic, being made

KIA-ORA the **fruit** squash

facturing 'artificial mineral waters' as early as the 1780s. As a lad he was considered too delicate for a life in agriculture and was placed with a silversmith. But he also took an interest in scientific affairs – in particular the aeration of water. Between 1790 and 1793 he attempted to introduce his drinks to the English market, but they got a poor reception to begin with. During the 1790s the term 'soda water' came into use, and in 1798, Schweppe's started to advertise its own brand. This was better received and was particularly recommended for the treatment of 'stone of the bladder'.

In 1831 the company moved to 51 Berners Street in London – an address which was to appear on millions of their famous egg-shaped bottles. At about this time they also received a royal warrant as soda and mineral water manufacturers. The *Illustrated London News* of 15 June 1844 carried a classified advertisement for 'Schweppe's Soda and Potass Waters, constantly used at the Royal Palaces at Windsor and London, as well as by the principal Nobility and Gentry of the United Kingdom, and recommended by all the leading medical

professions.' In 1835 Schweppe's Aerated Lemonade was introduced, and in the 1870s they added tonic water and ginger ale to their products, followed in 1931 by the introduction of an aerated orange drink. Over the years the company's advertising has been innovative, the famous line 'Schh . . . you know who' being perhaps their best-known slogan.

The story of Coca-Cola starts in Atlanta, Georgia, in 1886. It was there that pharmacist Dr John S. Pemberton first produced a syrup in a three-legged pot in his back yard. It was his partner, Frank Robinson, who suggested the name 'Coca-Cola', which he designed in a flowing script. At first the drink was very slow to take off; today sales exceed 600 million a day. Dr Pemberton did not realize the value of the product he had created and, when he was ill and in need of funds, he sold two friends a two-thirds interest for $1,220, including the sole right to manufacture the syrup. Four months before he died, in 1888, he and his son sold the remaining rights for $500. In the first year of the twentieth century Coca-Cola came to London, and its popularity quickly reached all parts of Britain.

The year 1955 saw the first canning of Coca-Cola, although the company by no means gave up on their uniquely shaped glass bottle. Rather, in 1960, a US Patent Office granted it a trademark. Advertising has always been a strength of the company, and they were the first people to feature Santa Claus in an advertisement complete with his now familiar red outfit. When the first Apollo astronauts returned from their moon flight they were greeted by a flashing sign in New York's Times Square which read 'Welcome back to Earth, Home of Coca-Cola.'

into England he came up with the brand name 'Corona', and by 1934 his company was operating from 79 factories and depots which covered most parts of England and Wales. Shops also started to stock Corona soft drinks. In 1958 the company became part of the Beecham Group and is now owned by Britvic.

Fred and Thomas Pickup worked in their uncle's soft-drink business, but in 1907 set up on their own in a joint venture in Portsmouth, selling half-gallon jars of brewed ginger beer and sarsaparilla. However, in 1910, Fred decided to move to Pudsey, near Leeds, where he bought a similar small business. Within two years he had also opened a factory in Bradford where, in addition to the traditional half-gallon jars, he was bottling in pint-sized, screw-topped, stone bottles. In 1919 Fred introduced a range of carbonated soft drinks. He realized that customers could not see the drinks until they were poured, and that this

It was in the first decade of the twentieth century that William Evans, a grocer from Porth in the Rhondda Valley, started bottling mineral water under the name of 'Welsh Hills Drinks'. In about 1912 he began a door-to-door delivery service, selling bread, tea and a range of drinks. Soon he expanded his business to include the whole of South Wales and Monmouthshire, and by 1925 was also covering North Wales. To assist him in his expansion

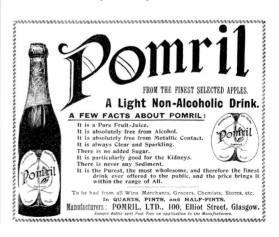

was a disadvantage. So, in 1920, he experimentally introduced pint-sized glass bottles – to much success. As his business prospered he opened yet another factory, this time in Manchester, and it was here, in 1924, that Tizer was launched – the name being coined from the word 'Appetizer', hence the catch phrase 'Tizer the Appetizer'.

Just before the First World War most towns had herbalist shops that sold hot and cold tonic drinks and cordials. These shops, and the temperance bars, were alternatives to pubs and billiard rooms. John Noel Nichols & Co of Manchester sold the ingredients for drinks such as dandelion-and-burdock, sarsaparilla and herb beer. About this time a Bill was going through Parliament to restrict the opening hours of public houses, and Nichols felt this presented an opportunity for the introduction of a branded soft drink. In 1908 he launched a fruit cordial which he claimed would give those who drank it 'vim and vigour'. Vimto was registered in 1912, at first listed as a 'medicine', but in 1913 it was relisted as 'a beverage for human use, not alcoholic, not aerated, and not medicated'.

Its popularity quickly spread throughout the country. In 1920 the syrup was adapted so that Vimto could be made into a sparkling drink, and in 1926 the cordial was bottled so that the public could make their own drinks at home. It also became available as pastilles, milk-shake syrup, and as an ice-cream topping. Future advertising in the 1950s and 60s stressed the part such drinks could play in encouraging 'safe driving', and the company made much of Vimto being 'A Drink for all the Family'.

During the Second World War the government issued children with orange juice and

rose-hip syrup as sources of vitamin C, and parents were encouraged to go out into the hedgerows and collect rose hips, which were then made into syrup at home. At school all children were also given a ⅓-pint bottle of milk each day.

In 1902 *Chambers's Journal* expressed concern that lemonade and other saccharine beverages were contaminated due to the use of acids, which gave metallic impurity, and today experts would advise us to cut out many soft drinks and stick to plain old water. However, caffeine lovers might be interested to know that when Voltaire was asked 'Is coffee bad for your health?' he replied: 'I have been poisoning myself for the last 80 years, but I'm not dead yet!'

Waste Not, Want Not!
SOUPS, SAUCES & LEFTOVERS

In earlier centuries the poor had to exist on a very meagre selection of foods. Hard bread and salted meat was the only sustenance many people got in medieval winters, which not only wore down the teeth, but led to such diseases as scurvy. For the literally starving, pittance, a soup made from dried peas, was offered at the convent door.

Soups and stews were the basis of most people's meals. To boiling water was added just about every available ingredient, from sheep's head, chicken carcass and oxtail, to bits and pieces of vegetable and barley – an ideal way of eking out scarcities, such as mutton and beef, and of using up leftovers. In many homes the stockpot was kept going for several days.

Today few of us have to try too hard with soup. When we take a tin of Heinz Tomato or Baxters Chicken Broth out of our cupboards, we can pour it into a mug to microwave in a minute, or into a saucepan to warm up in a very short time – and with some soups we need only add boiling water to the contents of a packet! For those who still like to make soup, ready-prepared stock cubes are usually only a reach away. It was not always thus. Many of us will find this Victorian recipe for common stock more than a little daunting:

Take about 3lbs shin of beef, seeing that the butcher does not send it all bone; put this into the stockpot with 2 large onions well fried, 2 raw onions, 2 large carrots cut down the centre, a head of celery, and a few sprigs of sweet herbs; add to this 3–4 quarts cold water, and set it on the fire to boil; let it remain boiling for 3–4 hours, draw it to the side, and let it simmer for the rest of the day; in the evening strain the liquor through a sieve into a large basin, put the

rest on a dish, set both in the larder, and have the stockpot well washed out before putting it away for the night. The next morning take the meat from the bones to use for potted meat, put the bones and vegetables into the stockpot, together with any bones large or small, left from the previous day, trimmings of meat, cooked or uncooked, gristle, skin, etc; bones from poultry and game of any kind should be used with the rest, and a ham or bacon bone, or trimmings from a tongue, all help to improve the flavour of the stock. Carefully skim the fat from the stock made yesterday, measure off as much as may be required for soup, gravies, etc. during the day, and pour the remainder into the stockpot, filling it up with cold water; freshly browned onion must be added every day, and every second or third day the vegetables must be changed for fresh ones. Every morning the bones, etc. must be looked over, taking away those in which no goodness remains as others are added. The water in which rice has been boiled, or in which bread has been soaked for puddings, should all go into the stockpot, and of course that which has been used in boiling fresh meat or poultry.

Not all soup was the preserve of the poor. Royal kitchens also kept their stockpots on the boil, though admittedly with a dash of finer ingredients. The creation of Windsor Soup is attributed to Charles Elme Francatelli, an Englishman of Italian extraction, who was chef to Queen Victoria at Windsor Castle. There are two versions of Windsor Soup, one a

In Victorian times, the explosion of population in rapidly-expanding industrial cities led to huge poverty amongst the working classes and many went hungry. Soup kitchens were set up to feed those who would otherwise starve, and offered such fare as scrap soup – a soup made from butcher's trimmings, bones, vegetables, crusts, bacon rind and water.

RIGHT: *Soup being served to the poor at the Half Penny Soup House in London, 1870.*

ABOVE: *Lewis Carroll created the fictional character of the Mock Turtle in his famous book* Alice in Wonderland.

of ham, two knuckles of veal, onions and a bottle of madeira.

Mock turtle soup is made, not of turtles, but as in a recipe of 1811, of '10 lbs of shin beef, 2 onions, half a calf's head, a very little flour, herbs, suet dumplings, and salt and pepper.' It was famously parodied in Lewis Carroll's *Alice in Wonderland*:

Then the Queen left off, quite out of breath, and said to Alice, 'Have you seen the Mock Turtle yet?'

'No,' said Alice. 'I don't even know what a Mock Turtle is.'

'It's the thing Mock Turtle Soup is made from,' said the Queen.

'I never saw one, or heard of one,' said Alice.

Such recipes were created to allow the less well-off to pretend they were enjoying the luxuries of a big house. Whilst it did not contain turtle, mock turtle soup was often served in a turtle shell. Today turtle soup and its counterfeit alternative have all but disappeared.

Baxters are renowned for their bestselling quality soups. In 1914, William and Ethel Baxter bought a plot of land from the Duke of Gordon and built a small factory on it. They specialized in the making of preserves. However, it is for their high-quality soups that they are perhaps best known. One night in 1929, William tripped over some sacks full of venison

consommé, the other a thick, brown soup, which is prepared from a pureé of rice enriched with calves'-foot jelly and thickened with cream and egg yolk. Curry powder is also known to have been added.

In the years following the First World War, the Adelphi Hotel in Liverpool had a pool containing turtles, which they used in the making of turtle soup. In *Mrs Beeton's Book of Household Management* we have a very graphic description of the various stages of making this soup, although few present day housewives (or househusbands) would relish the task of dismembering the turtle in the way she so clearly advises. Interestingly, in addition to a small turtle, Mrs Beeton's recipe includes six slices

from the local estate that had been left on the platform at Aviemore station. It occurred to him that there was potential in such an abundance of local game and he soon mentioned to his wife his idea for a game soup. Ethel was already an accomplished soup maker and was more

than happy to turn her preserve-making skills to soup making. Today the company, which is still family owned, is famous for its Royal Game Soup, and many others, such as Cock-a-Leekie, a chicken and leek soup.

The contents and origins of some soups can be confusing. Mulligatawny, for example, is a corruption of the Tamil for 'pepper water' – *milaku* being pepper and *tanni* water – for it is a hot, spicy soup containing curry, chicken or other meat. It is thought to have originated in the eighteenth century and was first brought to England by employees of the East India Company.

Cullen skink is a traditional Scottish soup using Finnan haddock and potatoes as its main ingredients. The first part of its name comes from the small fishing town of Cullen on the southern side of the Moray Firth, whereas the word 'skink' means 'cooked in a pot'. Cullen skink has long associations with the Seafield Hotel in Cullen, and haddock is still smoked in the nearby village of Buckie.

Many children who grew up in the war years, when food was scarce, will remember being told to finish what was on their plates before leaving the table. And if there were any leftovers from supper, these were not to be wasted. In Britain we have a host of traditional dishes such as shepherd's pie, cottage pie and bread-and-butter pudding that have evolved either from the need to waste not, want not, or from the need to stretch a supper further. Different regions have their own specific dishes. Ireland has its Irish stew and Lancashire its hotpot, for example. In Norfolk, a traditional dish is pork cheese, which is made from the leftovers of meat, which are mashed into a basin and the mixture left to set. When solid, the 'cheese' is turned out and sliced.

During the Second World War, when Lord Woolton was Minister for Food, an economical dish was devised, which became known as

ABOVE: *Lord Woolton visits a field kitchen during the Second World War.*

Woolton Pie. On the outside it was said to look exactly like a steak and kidney pie; however, the Imperial War Museum has a recipe for the pie and it has not a trace of steak or kidney.

Historically, or perhaps until the recent beef crisis, it has always been the case that as little as possible of an animal's carcass was wasted. We have probably all had occasion to eat 'humble pie'. However, few people know that this was once 'umble pie', which was made from umbles – the heart and liver of deer. Whilst umble pie is off today's menu, haggis, sausages, chitterlings, black pudding, oxtail, tongue and tripe are still popular.

Of course, where food is boring in taste, or bad, it has been important to enhance or disguise the original taste and smell. Although we have fewer of these sorts of problems today, most of us will have a space in our cupboards for sauces and relishes.

Lord Sandys, of the County of Worcester, had returned from India, where he had been Governor of Bengal. When visiting the East he had acquired a recipe for a sauce and now he wanted it made up. He approached Lea & Perrins of Broad Street in Worcester, who not only made the sauce for his lordship, but also got his permission to make a batch for themselves. However, when they tasted it, they found it so unpalatable that they put the jars in the cellar to gather dust. Some time later, when they were about to throw the jars away, one brave employee decided to have another taste. To much surprise, the sauce was found to have

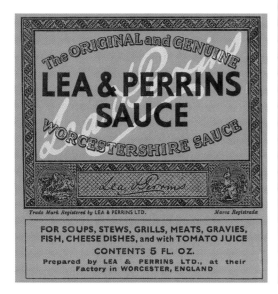

matured and was considered to be superlative. Thus Worcestershire Sauce came into being. Although today its ingredients have to be printed on its label, the original Worcestershire Sauce recipe and the required period of maturity have been kept a secret, and only a handful of people are party to the complete manufacturing process.

Mayonnaise was the late-eighteenth-century creation of the chef to the Duc de Richelieu, who, finding himself short of sauce ingredients during the siege of Port Mahon in Minorca, had to make do with mixing eggs and oil.

Henry Heinz was born in America in 1844 and when he was five moved to live near Pittsburgh. When he was sixteen he began to dry and grate horseradish and to sell it in clear glass bottles, so his customers could see what they were buying. Heinz ensured that his product was free from artificial preservatives and had no impurities or colouring – he even offered a money-back guarantee to his customers should they fail to be pleased with his

O.Ksauce

fruits and spice
and all things nice

HP in it

product. The company expanded its product list and Henry came up with the slogan '57 varieties'. His products actually numbered over sixty at this time, but the number appealed to him. In 1895 he produced his first can of baked beans in tomato sauce, and introduced Cream of Tomato Soup in 1910. Today the company sells 9 million cans of the soup each day.

Heinz Salad Cream, a mixture of spirit vinegar, egg yolk and cornflour, was actually the creation of Charles Hellen, in 1914, who was then the British general manager of Heinz. During the inter-war years Heinz adopted the slogan: 'There's a tang to living when there's a tang to what you eat.'

The word ketchup is said to derive from the word *koe-chiap* or *ke-tsiap* from the Amoy dialect of

COLMAN'S MUSTARD

Pickles in Patterns

*Just one example
of uniformity
in food preparation*

EXAMINE closely a jar of Heinz pickles. They look good to eat, yes—but note the arrangement of the contents. Everything placed just so.

Now look at another jar. It shows the same uniform pattern. You can't tell them apart. And any number of jars, each packed by a different girl, show the same orderly, tasteful arrangement.

The neat, prim, white-capped "Heinz girls" do this very skillfully and rapidly. Visitors to the Heinz spotless kitchens marvel at their deftness.

This uniformity in packing is proof of a still greater thing—the uniformity of the products which are packed. It speaks volumes for the care in sorting and selecting.

And the Heinz principle of uniformity goes still further. It is uniformity of grade and quality as well as of size—uniformity in every phase of preparation. Any one jar of pickles or any one can of beans is exactly as good as any other jar or can. The uniform quality and taste of each of the 57 Varieties is something which can always be depended upon.

The reason is not only high standards of food preparation—but cheerful loyalty to these standards by the men and women who do the preparing.

H. J. HEINZ COMPANY

57
Varieties

China, where it meant the brine of pickled fish. Alternatively, it could have originated from the Malayan word *kechap*, meaning sauce. The name was first known in Britain in about 1690 as 'catchup', later becoming 'catsup' and finally ketchup. Heinz began making ketchup in 1876 and the Heinz recipe has changed very little since. However, tomato sauces were being made and even bottled a long time before. Early adverts suggest the sauce should be eaten with meat, fish and poultry.

Thousand-Island dressing, the pink, mayonnaise-based salad dressing, which is flavoured with tomatoes, chili and green peppers, is said to take its name from the Thousand Islands, a group of small islands which are to be found in the St Lawrence River, along the Canadian–American border.

Yorkshire Relish was originally manufactured by Goodall, Backhouse & Co of Leeds. They started in business in 1853, and at the end of the nineteenth century they were selling 6 million bottles of it each year. They referred to their relish as being the 'most appetizing of sauces and most wholesome of digestive condiments. The piquancy and delicacy of this delicious preparation are universally appreciated, and gastronomes pronounce it equally good with fish, flesh and fowl.'

Mustard was introduced to Britain by the Romans, although it would have been produced from roughly crushed seeds of plants of the cabbage family, which were then mixed with unfermented grape juice – a very different mustard from the famous yellow jars of Colman's of Norwich. These began as little yellow tins of mustard powder in the nineteenth century. The earliest known reference to the now famous Bull's Head trademark was in 1855.

Béchamel sauce, a basic white sauce of flour, butter and milk, to which onion and seasonings are added, is said to have been invented by Louis de Béchameil, the Marquis de Niontel, who became Lord Steward in the royal household of Louis XIV of France. However, it is likely that the sauce was in existence under some other name before his time, and was somehow named after him.

Béarn, which is situated near the Atlantic coast on the French-Spanish border, is renowned for its cooking and particularly for Béarnaise sauce, which is said to have been created there and named in honour of King Henry IV, who was known as the Great Béarnais.

It is thought that the word 'OK' or 'okay' derives from the Choctaw Indian tribe word *hoke* or *oke*. Andrew B. Jackson, who later became President of the United States, is said to have used the word OK as

an abbreviation of the term 'all correct' in his 1789 senatorial campaign for the State of Tennessee. OK Sauce, however, was the creation of one H.W. Brand who was the royal chef to King George IV. Like most Hanoverians, George IV had a reputation as a great eater. Legend has it that during one of his huge twenty-course dinners, the king summoned his chef and said, 'Brand, this sauce is A1', to which Brand responded, 'With the greatest respect, Your Majesty, if it's A1 by you, it's OK by me.' Later, Brand began to sell his sauce as A1 Sauce. His nephews, George and John Mason, joined him in a business, but in 1880 they set up independently in a small factory in King's Road, Chelsea. They called their sauce OK Sauce. It was soon winning awards, even gaining a Gold Medal in Paris in 1888 and the highest Diploma in Vienna in 1890.

Vinegar dates back to Old Testament times, for in the book of Ruth we read 'And Boaz said unto her, At mealtime come thou hither, and eat of the bread, and dip thy morsel in the vinegar.' Edwin Samson Moore started the Midland Vinegar Company in 1875 in Aston, Birmingham, and, much to his wife's disgust, they made their home next door to the brewery. About this time, many families were returning from the various outposts of the British Empire, bringing with them recipes for spicy foods and sauces. Samson felt that the time was ripe to introduce a new sauce, but he realized the importance of having not only a good recipe but also a catchy name. One day he and his son went to call on one of his debtors, a Mr F. G. Garton of Nottingham. They were shown into a back room where a sauce was cooking in the washhouse copper. It was the basket-cart

standing in the yard that caught Samson's eye, however – on it were painted the words 'Garton's HP Sauce'. In a moment a deal was done and the debt was cancelled. Mr Garton claimed that his sauces were used in the Houses of Parliament and the building is featured on every label.

Walk around any supermarket today and you will see a wide choice of soups and sauces – all testament to successful marketing, branding and enterprise. However, we should not forget either their humble beginnings, original purpose, or their inspired originators.

Come into the Dairy
FARM FARE

People probably learnt to domesticate milk-producing animals around 6,000 to 8,000 BC, but it was only in the twentieth century that traditional milk-producing skills were success-

fully transferred to mass production in Europe and North America.

While milk from ewes and goats is known to be the richest in butterfat, and asses' or mares' milk the poorest (although mares' milk is high in sugar), cows' milk is the most plentiful and has therefore been the choice of commercial production. Before refrigeration, pasteurization and the development of good transport systems, producing milk for large populations and keeping it fresh was problematic. Arguably, rural areas had access to better quality milk, although even this could be easily contaminated. However, until the 1860s most town milk was provided by unhygienic

urban dairies, with ill-lit, unventilated byres and badly-drained yards. Some traders even kept cattle in stalls at the back of their shops. The quality of the cows and their foodstuffs was often poor, and their milk was frequently put into rusty, unscoured, open pails. When the milk was carried on a dray, it was not far from the rear end of the horse pulling it, and, being uncovered, was open to contamination from flies and dirt.

The first record of milk being carried in bulk from country to town was by train, in 1840, from Cheshire dairies to Manchester; although, maybe because railway networks covered only limited distances at this time, this mode of transportation did

not at first catch on. However, the demand for fresh milk in towns was rapidly increasing as populations quickly expanded during the industrial revolution. Milk was sometimes adulterated to make it go further. A roundsman running out of milk would be tempted to top up his pails from the 'iron cow' (the street water-pump) or, perhaps so that he could plead not guilty to adding water to the milk, he might put the water in first. The Victorian housewife or cook would test the freshness of a pail by licking her finger and then sticking it into the milk. If it was not warm, she would make the assumption that it had not come straight from the cow and was therefore unfit to drink; hardly a reliable or hygienic way of going about things, but that was how they reasoned in those days!

An 1852 issue of *Punch* stated that a clean glass of milk would be one of the seven wonders of London and asked if the capital

would have to wait until there was another February with five Sundays in it before such a glassful could be obtained – that would make the year 1922! Matters reached a head when, in 1866, there were outbreaks of cattle plague and people were forced to look again at how they could improve their milk supply.

One man who caught on to this was George Barham, later to become Sir George, the son of a London dairyman and the grandson of a dairy farmer from Battle in East Sussex. Barham had not followed in the footsteps of his father and grandfather but had taken up the trade of a carpenter and builder. His day's work began at dawn, but he was often finished by four o'clock in the afternoon. It was this work schedule that led the teenage Barham to notice how, each afternoon, some London cow-keepers would often have surplus milk,

while others would have difficulty supplying their customers' wants. He carried out a little research in the City and the Bloomsbury area of London and saw that there was an opening for a 'balancer' or middleman, who would resolve this problem. During the first few hours at the end of his working day he would take a dairymaid's traditional yoke, with five-gallon pails, and transport the milk from one supplier to another. Within a short space of time he had recruited an assistant porter, and by the time he was twenty the business had developed so much that he owned his own horse and a 'rully', a light, open-sided dray. Thus, in family tradition, he too had become a dairyman.

We know that at some time around the middle of the nineteenth century, 272 Strand passed into his ownership. In fact, there had been a dairy at this address since the seventeenth century and the building had at one time been linked with Nell Gwynne (1650-87). Supposedly, Nell was a milkmaid there, and there is a rumour that she and Charles II first met in the meadows that separated the dairy from nearby Whitehall Palace. Whether this was before she began selling oranges is unclear, and it is more likely that she became Charles's mistress when she went on the stage at Drury Lane.

We also know that in 1858 Barham bought a shop, which he turned into his own dairy, although no cows were kept there. It was at the extreme west end of the City, in Dean Street, off Fetter Lane. However, by the early 1860s George Barham had started to use bulk supplies of milk, delivered by train from outlying dairy farms, to supplement his local supplies. The dairies were not actually very far away; in fact they were probably not far from Holborn, so the milk would arrive still fresh for delivery. By 1864 Barham had realized that in this method of bringing in milk lay the foundations of a whole new enterprise.

By now, express trains were bringing milk into King's Cross and, keen to maximize the advantages this offered, George purchased new premises in nearby Museum Street. He soon named his business 'The Express Country Milk Supply Company'. It was the start of Express Dairies.

Others were also looking at ways in which to improve milk production. The need for a good milking machine was advocated, but farmers treated the idea with mistrust; many thought it might be injurious to the cow and would result in poorer quality milk. The earliest devices for mechanical milking were wooden tubes inserted in the cows' teats, although feather quills were also used. There were many patents given out for milking machines. Messrs. Lawrence and Kennedy patented one

LEFT: *Express Dairies delivery vehicles.*
FACING PAGE ABOVE: *A roundsman with his milk cart.*
FACING PAGE BELOW: *Loading an early milk float at Express Dairies.*

such in 1900, which was designed to be powered by electricity, oil, gas, steam or water. They also patented a new hand-milking machine.

Emperor Napoleon III asked French chemist Louis Pasteur to investigate the diseases afflicting wine, which were causing considerable economic losses to the wine industry. Pasteur went to a vineyard in Arbois in 1864

to study the problem. He demonstrated that wine diseases are caused by micro-organisms that can be killed by heating the wine to 55 degrees centigrade for several minutes. Applied to beer and milk, this process, now called 'pasteurization', soon came into use throughout the world. It was a breakthrough in improving the standard of milk.

Unless we forget to buy it, few of us have problems getting fresh milk on to our tables today. Most people probably buy their milk in supermarkets, but others still prefer their daily pint to be delivered from the milkman. Unigate Dairies deliver 2 million bottles of milk to our doorsteps every day – the produce of 150,000 cows.

There are occasions when the production of sour and curdled milk is to be encouraged, indeed stimulated. Cheese making is one such example. Cheese has been

made in Britain for centuries, even as far back as Roman times, and some types have survived the passing of time, becoming an established part of our heritage.

There are many different ways of producing cheese, and many different influencing factors, including milk type, local vegetation, climate and the time allotted for the cheese to mature; generally the longer a cheese is allowed to mature, the harder it will be. Commonly, cheese

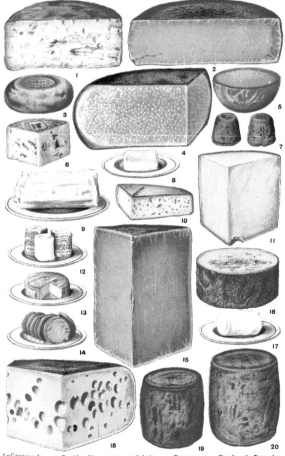

1 –Gorgonzola. 2—Double Gloucester. 3—Koboko. 4—Parmesan. 5 – Dutch. 6—Roquefort. 7—Schabzieger. 8—Dunragit. 9—York Cream. 10—Port du Salut. 11—Cheddar. 12 – Pommel. 13—Camembert. 14- Mainzer. 15—Cheshire. 16—Stilton. 17—Cream Bondon. 18—Gruyère. 19—Wiltshire Loaf. 20—Cheddar Loaf.

is made from curd, which is formed by adding rennet to milk. After the curd has been curdled, cut and ripened, it is transferred to a cheesecloth and hung to allow the whey to drain off. The curd is then packed into moulds or hoops and pressed down to consolidate. Many cheeses are then wrapped before being put into store to mature. This process was no doubt discovered by accident, but cheese is something many people would not be without today. It is said in some parts of the north of England that a slice of apple pie without some cheese is like a cuddle without a kiss!

Farmhouse cheeses were almost always made by women, although it was a physically demanding job. It was commonly said that 'the bigger the dairymaid, the better the cheese'! The pails of milk and water were heavy, the cutting of the curd was hard work and the 40-lb cheeses were difficult to lift and wrap. Individual cheese makers had their own secret recipes, which were passed down from one generation to another, and villages ran competitions to see which of the local farms produced the best cheese. At one time low-fat, skimmed-milk cheese was the most commonly consumed, with full-fat cheeses being something of a luxury and supplied to the local gentry.

It is believed that Cheshire cheese is the oldest of the English regional cheeses, dating back to local Celtic tribes. The Domesday Book has records of Norman ladies making Cheshire cheese, although normally such tasks would have been regarded as menial and would have been undertaken by the local village women. The Normans must have held this cheese in particularly high regard! Traditionally, Cheshire cheese is made at farms in the hills and dales

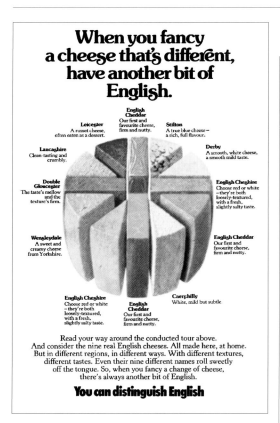

When you fancy a cheese that's different, have another bit of English.

English Cheddar
Our first and favourite cheese, firm and nutty.

Leicester
A russet cheese, often eaten as a dessert.

Stilton
A true blue cheese – a rich, full flavour.

Lancashire
Clean-tasting and crumbly.

Derby
A smooth, white cheese, a smooth mild taste.

Double Gloucester
The taste's mellow and the texture's firm.

English Cheshire
Choose red or white – they're both loosely-textured, with a fresh, slightly salty taste.

Wensleydale
A sweet and creamy cheese from Yorkshire.

English Cheddar
Our first and favourite cheese, firm and nutty.

English Cheshire
Choose red or white – they're both loosely-textured, with a fresh, slightly salty taste.

English Cheddar
Our first and favourite cheese, firm and nutty.

Caerphilly
White, mild but subtle.

Read your way around the conducted tour above.
And consider the nine real English cheeses. All made here, at home.
But in different regions, in different ways. With different textures,
different tastes. Even their nine different names roll sweetly
off the tongue. So, when you fancy a change of cheese,
there's always another bit of English.

You can distinguish English

helped out those farmers who were not gifted cheese makers by buying their excess milk and taking it to small factories, where they made it into cheese themselves. Thus a flourishing industry developed across the dales.

However, during the Depression of the early 1930s, Wensleydale's fortunes took a turn for the worse. In 1935, Kit Calvert, seeing the plight of the local cheese industry, called a meeting in the town hall of the small market town of Hawes. As a result of this meeting some dales' folk decided to form their own company, the 'Wensleydale Cheese Joint Conference', made up of cheese-factory managers, farmhouse cheese makers and cheese factors, who all worked together to save the industry.

For many Yorkshire folk, Christmas would not be the same without a slice of Wensleydale cheese to accompany their Christmas cake, and sales of the cheese have traditionally been at their highest in November and December. Prior to the outbreak of the Second World War, many thousands of 1-lb and 2-lb 'small' cheeses were produced for the Christmas market.

of Cheshire, North Shropshire and Clwyd. Salt, which naturally permeates the soils in these areas, helps to produce its characteristically crumbly texture. Predictably, the cheese has a slightly salty as well as a full-bodied flavour. It comes in red, white and blue types – a very patriotic cheese!

In Yorkshire, cheese was first made by monks in the abbeys of Wensleydale. Later, farmers' wives carried on the tradition, often bartering cheeses in exchange for groceries or corn for the animals. Making the cheese requires careful attention so that the curd does not turn sour. Thus some farms produced better cheese than others. Cheese factors

Something extra special for your lips this Christmas.

The Milk Marketing Board purchased the main Wensleydale creamery at Hawes, but in 1992 its subsidiary, Dairy Crest, wanted to transfer the making of Wensleydale to Lancashire. The War of the Roses nearly broke out again, for Yorkshire folk were not prepared to accept such a decision. Following a successful management buy out, the cheese remained safely in Yorkshire and today both the blue and the white Wensleydale are a thriving concern.

The Gloucesters are ancient cheeses but the Single or Double Gloucester we know today only became popular at the beginning of the eighteenth century, when advances in toughening the cheese rind for better keeping and improvements in the appearance of the cheese made for better sales.

Red Leicester was very popular in London during Victorian times. Its deep orange colour was obtained by adding a dye made from a carrot extract, but today its colour comes from the addition of a modern dye called annatto.

How strange that Stilton, a Leicestershire cheese, gets its name from a village in Huntingdonshire! Some say that a cream cheese made at Quenby Hall in Leicestershire, which was commonly known as Lady Beaumont's cheese, was the original Stilton cheese and that the recipe was passed on to the Paulet family. In the early 1700s a Mrs Paulet of Wymondham in Leicestershire, made a cream cheese, which she sent to Cooper Thornhill, a relation of hers who was the landlord of The Bell Inn at Stilton. The inn was situated on the Great North Road between London and Edinburgh, and gradually travellers spread the word about the highly-favourable cheese that was to be had in Stilton. The Stilton Cheese Makers Association was granted the use of Stilton as a trademark in 1966 and today the name Stilton can only be applied to cheeses of that type made in Leicestershire, Derbyshire and Nottinghamshire. In Blue Stilton, a mould belonging to the penicillin type grows naturally in the cheese, probably originally caused by damp dairy conditions, which were ideal for mould growing. White Stilton is sold before the veining has had time to develop.

The story of Cheddar cheese goes back to the fifteenth century when this popular cheese was first made in Somerset – particularly round the village of Cheddar. It was certainly

FACING PAGE ABOVE RIGHT: *The opening of the cheese market at Chippenham in 1850.*
RIGHT: *Butter and cream making, 1905.*

considered an excellent cheese during the Elizabethan period and farmers kept their recipes a tight secret. However, in the seventeenth century, farmers in the Cheddar district worked on a co-operative basis and their collective milk output was taken to one large dairy. A lively cheese trade developed as a result, both nationwide and abroad. Author Daniel Defoe observed, 'The whole village of Cheddar are cow-keepers'. Indeed, the Shorthorn cows were vital to the local economy, as these cows gave milk that was ideal for making cheese. It was once claimed that the locally-made cheeses were stored and matured in the caves that stretch under the Mendip Hills, where there was ideal humidity and evenness of temperature. A part of the cheese-making process is actually called 'cheddaring', which is the stage when the curds are turned and stacked in such a way as to speed up the draining of the whey. This was introduced in the nineteenth century by Joseph Harding whose slogan was: 'Cheese is not made in the field, nor in the byre, nor even in the cow – it is made in the dairy.' Cheddar should have a nutty, yet sharp flavour, although the taste will vary according to how long it is matured. Generally, the longer the cheese is allowed to mature, the fuller the flavour. The traditional rounds weigh 56 lbs. Since the middle of the nineteenth century most Cheddar has been made in factories, called creameries. Today, the cheese is made all over the country, although it is still made on some Cheddar farms. Cheddar is the nation's favourite cheese, accounting for nearly 60 per cent of sales, the stronger flavours being preferred to the mild ones.

While Scotland has such cheeses as Caithness, Orkney, Islay and Dunlop, Wales has the smooth Caerphilly. Caerphilly is quite a young cheese, being less than two hundred years old, and takes its name from the Welsh village of the same name. It proved so popular in the late nineteenth century that Welsh farmers could not cope with demand and they asked their English neighbours, the Cheddar farmers, to help them out. As Caerphilly requires much less ripening time than Cheddar, they were pleased to do so, and today most Caerphilly is made in England.

Delicious!

6d. per packet. At all Grocers.

Full fat soft cheese.

Cheese is found in nearly every part of the world. While many of us would not be familiar with reindeer cheese from Lapland, many of us enjoy Continental cheeses. Edam and Gouda are the best known of the Dutch cheeses. Parmesan and Gorgonzola are both Italian cheeses; the latter, coming from the Lombardy region, is made from full milk, traditionally while still warm from the cows. Roquefort is a French cheese originally made from sheep's milk or from both sheep and goats' milk. Camembert, originally from Britanny, and Gruyère, originally from a town to the east of Lausanne in Switzerland, are now made outside their original regions and thus their character and quality can vary considerably. However, Brie, which has been eaten since at least the thirteenth century and has been crowned *Roi des Fromages* can still only be made successfully in a small number of French towns.

It is said by some that the distribution of milk by railways destroyed the unique flavour

of many individual farm cheeses. Certainly, some once famous cheeses such as Oxford, Suffolk, the Blue Cottenham from Cambridge and the Daventry have disappeared, while others such as the Dorset Blue Vinney are now quite rare.

Historically, butter has had many uses, as a cosmetic, an ointment, a lubricant and even as lamp fuel. There are two types of butter: lactic and sweetcream. In general, lactic butters are either slightly salted or unsalted. Sweetcream butter is salted and is the preferred butter throughout most of Britain. The best butter was once produced in mid-summer when the cows had grazed fully on the spring grass; it was a rich golden-yellow in colour, but its flavour would depend on the skill of the individual dairymaid. It was often sold in stone-built buttermarkets, which were cool, and many are still to be found in the centre of towns across the country. While today it is held up as a fatty substance that is not good for us, in earlier days butter was used generously, not just on bread but as a sauce on stews, herbs, vegetables and fish.

Butter is normally made from the fatty milk of the cow known as butterfat, which is churned until it solidifies, although it can be made from the milk of goats, sheep and other milk-producing animals. The sourish liquid that is left in the pail when the creamier milk is removed is known as buttermilk and is often used for making scones and soda bread. Jersey and Guernsey cows give milk that is rich in butterfat. However, for many decades much of our butter was imported from New Zealand, although this supply has been partly eroded

since Britain joined the European Community.

Henry Reynolds was a Cornishman who emigrated to New Zealand and built a butter factory at Waikato, where, on 3 November 1886, he made his first 'churning'. Why he chose Anchor as the brand name we do not know – maybe for an early settler its symbolism of safe arrival would be important. Ten years later he sold his company and the brand name to the New Zealand Dairy Association. Over the years further amalgamations took place and the New Zealand Dairy Company was formed. In 1924 they started pre-packing the butter to encourage customers to choose the Anchor brand. This was an innovative idea as, prior to the Second World War, most housewives bought their butter from a large block, which was on display on the counter, and generally unprotected from

A fine example of the art of butter making

DAIRY HERDS grazing out of doors the whole year round produce the rich cream for the expert buttermakers of New Zealand to churn into butter of fine quality and flavour – with all the natural goodness that springs from fresh green pasturelands.

Although New Zealand is the world's greatest exporter of butter and cheese, dairy farmers are all out to increase production still further.

NEW ZEALAND BUTTER

BUTTER AT ITS VERY BEST

dirt, flies or heat. By 1969 Anchor was the most popular brand of butter on sale in Britain.

In the middle of the nineteenth century many people could not afford butter and as a result their diets lacked adequate levels of fat. In France, Napoleon III encouraged the search for a suitable replacement among chemists and in 1867 Mege Mouries suggested a combination of kidney fat churned with milk and sliced udders – it doesn't sound at all desirable! However, it caught on, initially as butterine, but as this

angered butter producers, the name margarine was adopted; it was believed, erroneously, that the spread contained a fatty acid called margaric acid. It is actually debatable whether margarine improved nutrition – for it lacked the vitamin and nutritional value of butter and therefore no doubt exacerbated the malnutrition of the poor.

Tub margarines and vegetable-oil spreads were introduced in the 1960s. Over the years non-butter spreads have been developed for particular purposes, some being suitable for use in making cakes, while others are used mainly for spreading on bread. Recently, many new products have appeared on the market as consumers continue to search for 'healthy' spreads. Today, Unigate's St Ivel produces around 150 million tubs of margarine and dairy spreads each year.

Ice cream, properly made from cream and egg yolks, but often made from milk or a custard base, is an enjoyable treat on a hot day. Today there is a vast range, from tubs of standard vanilla to the more exciting flavours produced by Häagen-Dazs and Ben & Jerry – not to mention choc-ices, Cornettos and the '99' ice cream cone with the chocolate flake. However, back in 1888 there was great concern that Italian immigrants, who sold chestnuts in winter and a cheap ice cream called 'hokey-pokey' in

summer, were using bad water and sour milk flavoured with acids, rather than with lemon juice, to make ice cream. Ice cream was reportedly being made in 'filthy dens' and was contained in dangerous leaden pots.

In 1894 *Chambers's Journal* reported that ice-cream vendors were spreading germs by the unhygienic way in which they dealt with the eggs going into ice cream. Instead of breaking the shells in a normal manner, they were piercing them at each end and blowing the insides into a bowl. The reason for this was that the eggshells were then sold to shooting galleries for sportsmen to have 'the pleasure of smashing them from afar'.

Wall's is still our best known national brand of ice cream, but it all really started with Thomas Wall. His grandfather had taken over a meat-and-pie business in central London in 1806. By the time Thomas became involved in the business the company was making daily deliveries of pies and sausages to the royal palaces, and to the homes of other influential customers. However, at this time commercial methods of refrigeration were still in their infancy and it wasn't easy to keep their prod-

ucts fresh, especially during the warm months of the year. Indeed, there was a superstition that you should not eat meat if there was not an 'r' in the month. Thus, Wall's sales plummeted during May, June, July and August.

In 1922 the company decided to produce ice cream as an alternative product to help them through this summer period, a challenge to the Italians' monopoly of the street market. At that time Wall's supplied Macfisheries shops with pies and sausages, and Wall's tried to persuade them that they should also sell ice cream. However, Macfisheries did not want to be bothered with it. Butchers outlets the company tried felt similarly. Unfortunately, such was Wall's confidence in their idea that they were already producing 150 gallons of ice cream a week, prepacked in hand-wrapped, sandwich-size briquettes. What was to be done?

It was Fred Wall, Thomas's brother, who came up with the solution – why not buy a trike? At first the idea did not find favour with other members of the family, but in the end a trike was purchased for £6 and was duly loaded

BELOW LEFT: *'Hokey-pokey' street salesman.*
BELOW RIGHT: *Ice-cream sales by tricycle.*

WHEN YOU'RE OUT AND ABOUT

HAVE A WALLSIE

GOOD AND BIG!

BUY IT WHERE YOU SEE

THE (Wall's) SIGN

with ice and the ice-cream briquettes. Its first trip was around the streets of Acton, west London, where the company now had their factory. The trike carried no advertising, but the employee riding it had a good voice, and soon the slogan, 'Stop me and buy one', became a household phrase. By 1939 Wall's had 8,000 trikes on the road, operating from 136 depots.

The first choc-ice was launched in America in 1921. Wafer Ice Creams were introduced in 1905 by an ice-cream seller called Lewis in Bolton market. Ice-cream cones were first seen in Britain in 1910 and were introduced by Lawrence Askey. The first chiming ice-cream van made its rounds in 1951.

Yoghurt is a semi-solid, fermented milk product that originated centuries ago and is said to have been originally eaten by nomads in Persia and Asia Minor. However, it wasn't until the early 1900s that the rest of the world started to consider the value of yoghurt. Professor Elie

Metchnikoff, a Russian biologist working at the Pasteur Institute in Paris, was looking for a remedy for premature ageing. He felt that the reason for ageing lay with putrefying bacteria that remained in the large intestine and thereby poisoned the body. He looked at longevity statistics from many countries and discovered that in Bulgaria there was a connection between long life and people who ate yoghurt. The vital factor was an acid-forming organism, *Lactobacillus bulgaricus*. His work was noticed by Titus Barham, the son of George, founder of Express Dairies, who imported some of the *bacillus* and began producing yoghurt.

In the 1920s devotees of health foods claimed that yoghurt could not only prolong life, but also tighten flabby stomach muscles, correct weight gain and restore hair (it hasn't worked for me!).

Although milk from various animals has been used for yoghurt production, most industrialized yoghurt uses cow's milk. Over three million pots of yoghurt, fromage frais and chilled desserts are consumed in the UK each year.

Fruit-flavoured yoghurts were introduced into Britain in 1963. Paul Kewan had enjoyed some on a holiday in Switzerland and started to manufacture 'real fruit' yoghurts – almost at

once Britons were hooked. Today strawberry is the nation's favourite flavour, followed by raspberry and peach.

Traditionally, eggs have been regarded as a dairy product. Today all eggs are sold in their shells, and these must be free from cracks, although I remember how, about thirty years ago, we used to go to a smallholding and buy cracked eggs at a much-reduced price. We were never ill as a result of eating them, but today hygiene standards are higher.

Hen's eggs are by far the most commercial and, even in Victorian times, were available all year round, although they were often too expensive for poorer people in towns to afford. Duck eggs could only be had in early summer, and in parts of Norfolk and Yorkshire, the eggs of certain seagulls were also eaten. They were said to be the 'game' of eggs, having a rather unusual flavour.

Eggs have been imported into Britain since the beginning of the nineteenth century, reaching almost 3,000 million a year in the late 1930s. Many came from Denmark and Holland, as well as from such Commonwealth countries as Australia, Canada and South Africa. In earlier days eggs came from abroad in long cases, packed in straw, each case holding a 'long hundred', that being 120 eggs, to cover for breakages in transit; although these were generally few due to the skill of the packers. At the end of the nineteenth century eggs were shipped from Australia, having been placed in cold-store, and then packed in boxes with cardboard divisions, filled up with dry pea-husks. They arrived in this country between November and January, when British eggs were scarce.

In the war years it was also necessary to buy 'dried egg' powder when fresh eggs were in short supply.

It used to be said that a fresh egg took half a minute longer to boil than a stale one. However, around 1960 eggs were marked with a 'lion' stamp, which was a surer indication of quality. Various grading systems have been adopted over the years to indicate size and source of origin. Nowadays, for example, many people want to know that their eggs are free range.

Dairy products are essential to many of our culinary favourites, from custard to milkshake to cream cakes. And we are still striving for better and safer products, whether through European laws or many people's rediscovered preference for traditional, organic and home-farm products.

Add an egg
You can rely on the lion

It's easy to melt 1 oz. of plain chocolate with a teaspoonful of water. (Per person)

It's easy to stir in a lion egg yolk (off the heat). And when cool add the white, stiffly beaten. (One egg per person)

for <u>real</u> chocolate mousse

It's easy to pop it into a dish and eat it creamy-cold next day.

Getting Off to a Good Start
CEREALS

Ceres was the Roman goddess of agriculture, but today is remembered in our daily helping of 'cereals'. Dr Johnson wrote under the word oat, in his dictionary of 1755, 'In Scotland it supports the people, but in England is generally given to horses'. Oats will produce an economic crop even in cold, wet areas where other cereals might fail, and that includes the Scottish Highlands.

Before the days of 'refined' porridge oats, porridge was a very variable breakfast food. In *Spon's Household Manual* of 1891 they suggest the following recipe:

Put on a fire a pan, of the size that will hold the quantity required, about ⅔ full of water; when the water is quick boiling take a handful of meal, and holding the hand over the pan – of course high enough to avoid being burned by the steam – let the meal slide slowly through the fingers into the water, the other hand stirring all the time with a wooden spoon. Continue this till enough of meal is put into the water, then add salt to taste, and, allow the porridge to boil for 20–30 minutes, stirring occasionally lest it stick to the pan and scorch. Porridge is not good if boiled less than 20 minutes; but for children or delicate stomachs it should be boiled the full ½ hour, by which time the meal is so

well swelled and softened that it becomes a digestible and most nutritious article of food. If the meal is thrown in too quickly, or the water allowed to cease boiling, it forms into lumps and is not so good.

Today, few of us have this much time to devote to our breakfasts; we want some-

thing which is quicker, more reliable, and possibly with milk and sugar added, rather than salt.

Unfortunately, no one seems to know who A. & R. Scott were who first branded Scott's Porage Oats, but the company behind the cereal was soon leading the way in its hygienic methods of food preparation. The two Scott brothers started making Midlothian Oat Flour in Glasgow in 1880 and as early as 1884 *The Mercantile Age* was reporting on the excellent facilities at their mill. At that time they were packing about one thousand 1-lb tins each day – some of them bound for the West Indies, America, New Zealand and various parts of the Continent. However, the factory was fully mechanized and none of the contents was touched by human hand. All containers were hermetically sealed. Oats for

porage were milled on the uppermost floor of the factory, while on the ground floor there was a bakery where oatcakes and biscuits were 'fired'. It was in 1914 that they introduced the term 'Scott's Porage Oats' and it is still their registered trademark today. 'Porage' is a combination of the old Scottish word *poray* and the French word *potage*. The Scottish Highlander putting the shot was added to the packaging in 1924.

Far away in the United States, at Battle Creek, near Michigan, the minister's wife at the Seventh Day Adventist Church believed that a diet based on grains, nuts and foods of vegetable origin was essential to 'right living'. As a result, the Western Health Reform Institute was formed at Battle Creek. In 1876 Dr John Harvey

Waiter's Smile.

If Quaker Oats the order be
This waiter's sure he'll get a fee,
And so upon his face we see
The smile that won't come off!

Kellogg was appointed its chief physician. He developed an easy-to-digest breakfast for the patients, replacing the rather heavy, traditional morning meal that was then widely eaten. With his brother, William Keith, he developed paper-thin, malt-flavoured, toasted flakes of maize (also known as Indian corn), and the cereal was so popular that former patients requested regular supplies be posted to them.

In 1906 William Keith Kellogg established the Battle Creek Toasted Corn Flake Company in a small wooden building in the town, but after about a year it was destroyed by fire. However, he was not deterred and built a larger and better plant at which he established rigid quality controls for all stages of production. To avoid confusion with his competitors, W. K. Kellogg had his signature printed on every packet, and for many years the packet also carried the slogan 'The original bears the signature'. Today the cereal is colloquially referred to as 'Kelloggs' or 'cornflakes'. By the 1930s they had pioneered nutritional labelling, and by the 1950s Kelloggs had introduced such cereals as All Bran, Special K and Rice Krispies – with its never-to-be-forgotten Snap, Crackle and Pop!

An American of Welsh descent, Charles William Post went to Battle Creek to convalesce after a serious illness. Whilst there he started experimenting to produce a new cereal beverage. He had the use of a small barn, a petrol stove, a coffee grinder and a small quantity of grain. He called his drink Monk's Brew, but later changed it to Postum Cereal. Although still a sick man, on New Year's day 1895, Charles went to the Michigan food stores by horse and buggy and tried to sell his new product. Eventually it became popular as a winter drink, but Post wanted to create a product that had all-year-round appeal. In 1897 he introduced Grape-Nuts – a breakfast cereal made of baked wheat and malted barley, which had a nutty flavour. He also believed that grape sugar was formed during the baking process, hence the name Grape-Nuts. He later introduced a cereal called Elijah's Manna, but although people liked the taste they didn't like the name and he therefore changed it to Post Toasties.

About this time an American lawyer, Henry D. Perkey of Denver, Colorado, was

"You're right..
WELGAR
SHREDDED WHEAT
and FRUIT is delicious"

Of all cereals, Welgar Shredded Wheat is the natural partner of fruit. Serve it with bananas, stewed apples or plums, or any fruit in season. The family will love it!
Remember, Welgar Shredded Wheat is the best cereal with hot or warm milk, but it's equally delicious with cold milk, and a little sugar, syrup, honey or jam. Take a packet home today!

Summer ripened wheat
for Winter weather

Weetabix will keep them warm *inside*

Keeping them warm all day in winter depends not so much on hot food as on the sort of food they eat. And one of the finest foods for keeping out the cold is delicious golden Weetabix. Summer-ripened wheat; malt; sugar — Weetabix provides natural warmth-giving goodness in its most tempting form. So start each winter's day with Weetabix and help keep the family fighting fit. With hot milk or cold, with marmalade or fried with bacon, it's the warmth *in* Weetabix that counts.

Weetabix
the whole wheat breakfast cereal

Out·of·this·world !

Happy families *everywhere* love
Kellogg's SUGAR FROSTED FLAKES

Never mind the weather—take no notice of gloomy mornings. They all turn to gold when the pack of Sugar Frosted Flakes appears on the table. Luscious large golden flakes of corn dipped in pure sugar till they sparkle and glitter —no wonder they're irresistible! Try them today, and see for yourself!

The most delicious breakfast you *ever* tasted!

lunching at a country inn when he observed another customer eating some boiled whole wheat, mashed up with cream. Striking up a conversation with the customer, Henry discovered that they both suffered from chronic dyspepsia. However, his newfound friend informed him that the food he was now enjoying relieved his indigestion, as well as other ailments from which he suffered. Henry Perkey turned his back on his law firm and set about developing an easy-to-eat, healthy cereal. He produced a machine that pressed wheat into shred-like shapes, which, when baked, made delicious biscuits. Perkey named his new food product Shredded Wheat. At first he tried selling his shredding machines, but soon discovered that people preferred to purchase the ready-made biscuits. He built factories at Boston and Niagara Falls and soon Shredded Wheat was being described as the world's first ready-to-eat cereal, with the added attractions of being high in fibre but free from sugar or salt.

Shredded Wheat was first imported into Britain in 1908 and the factory at Welwyn Garden City was opened in 1926. In 1928 the company was acquired by the American National Biscuit Company which became Nabisco after the Second World War. In 1953 the company introduced Shreddies, and now also makes such products as Bitesize Shredded Wheat, Golden Grahams and Cheerios. Today the company is part of the larger Cereal Partners UK, who are based at Watford and produce the Force brand range of cereals.

The Force Company of Buffalo in America was launched in 1901, one of just scores of cereal companies founded around that time. However, rather than being promoted as a breakfast cereal, the aim was to encourage people to eat it at any time of day, its vitamins giving a quick supply of energy. In 1903 the Force Company began a new advertising campaign and introduced Sunny Jim, a character created by Minnie Maud Hanff and Dorothy Ficken. Jim Dumps, initially a morose fellow, became transformed by 'Force' and became

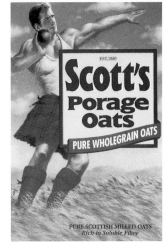

EST.1880
Scott's Porage Oats
PURE WHOLEGRAIN OATS

PURE SCOTTISH MILLED OATS
Rich in Soluble Fibre

Sunny Jim. Many types of products were produced to reinforce the message, including the now very collectible Sunny Jim dolls.

Weetabix, unlike many of the other breakfast cereals, is of British origin. Launched in the 1930s, it is made from whole-wheat grain, so contains natural fibre, as well as providing carbohydrates, protein, 'B' vitamins and iron. Today, Weetabix Ltd is based at Burton Latimer in Northamptonshire and at Corby, and produces over 70 million breakfast biscuits a week from home-grown wheat. The company also produces Ready Brek, the instant, hot, oat cereal, and Alpen.

Muesli is a Swiss dish consisting of cereal, fruit and nuts. It was introduced into Britain in 1926, at first only being eaten by those who made purchases from health-food shops. In its early days in Britain, it was sometimes called

company, was established in Britain, and in 1936 a production unit was opened in Southall. Puffed Wheat was introduced in 1907 and Puffed Rice in 1910. Post-war products have included Sugar Puffs, in 1954, and Oat Crunchies in 1957. Quaker Oats and also Scott's Porage Oats are now both produced at the mill at Cupar in Scotland, whilst the company's ready-to-eat products and cereal snack bars are produced at Southall.

Of course, the traditional English breakfast is a good fry-up and many people still like this breakfast best, even if they reserve it for holidays and weekends. Still, there is no doubt that in Britain we consume a large amount of breakfast cereals, and benefit from their vitamins and fibre, even if, these days, many of them are a little less healthy than Dr Kellogg and his fellow pioneers might wish.

Birchermuesli, after Dr Bircher-Benner who served it to patients at his 'natural health' clinic in Zurich.

In 1850 John Stuart left the Scottish highlands to begin a new life in Canada. Initially he acquired an old oat mill, which produced about 25 barrels of oatmeal a day. Later, he and his son Robert moved to Cedar Rapids in Iowa, where they built a new mill, and, in association with other local people, developed a substantial business. In 1877 they registered their trademark, Quaker Oats, the first trademark to be registered for a breakfast cereal. They felt the Quakers, with their purity of living, honesty and strength of character, embodied the qualities they wished to adopt. In line with this thinking, the original trademark depicted a man in full Quaker outfit carrying a scroll bearing the word 'Pure'. In later years the Quaker on the packaging became more robust and cheerful, but still symbolized the virtues of tradition and honesty. In 1899, Quaker Oats Ltd, a subsidiary

Ripe for Picking
FRUIT & VEGETABLES

Apples, pears, plums, gooseberries, strawberries and even pineapples have long been delicacies of British tables. Some, of course, like cherries, are native to Britain, while others have more exotic origins. The Romans introduced us to such fruits as figs and grapes, yet, in medieval times, not many people had tasted blackcurrants, for example, and only a few monastic gardens cultivated strawberries, which grew wild. Medlars, small trees that bear

FRUIT.

1.—Apricots. 2.—White Cherries. 3.—Black Cherries. 4.—White Currants.
5.—Black Currants. 6.—Red Currants. 7.—Melon. 8.—Strawberries. 9.—Raspberries.
10.—Plums (Black Diamonds). 11.—Greengages. 12.—Victoria Plums.

fruit similar to the crab apple, are mentioned in thirteenth-century literature, and in 1327 one Lord Berkeley sent his mother-in-law a dish of pears.

Oranges originally grew wild in India and China. Bitter Seville oranges were probably the first to arrive in Britain, via Spain, in the thirteenth century, but they were only suitable for pies or marmalade. By the fourteenth and fifteenth centuries they were quite cheap to buy. The orange is thought to take its name from the town of Orange in south-east France, a centre for trade in the fruit, although the fruit was known by other names before this. The concept of the colour orange probably dates from the fourteenth century and the old French word *auranja*. The more popular, sweeter oranges arrived in Britain in the seventeenth century, from Portugal. Originally called China Oranges, they would be the type sold by Nell Gwynne and other orange-sellers to theatregoers in London.

The story of Outspan, one of the well-known brand names associated with oranges, goes back to the time of Jan van Riebeck, the first

governor of the Cape of Good Hope. Realizing
the importance of oranges for the good health
of sailors who visited the port (their Vitamin C
preventing diseases such as scurvy) he sent a
small sailing ship to the little island of St
Helena, a journey of 2,000 miles, to bring back
suitable plants. These orange trees flourished
and from them today's oranges have grown.
The early settlers from Holland, France and
England had travelled across their new land
in ox-drawn, covered wagons. At night these
were arranged in circles to protect the people
from wild animals – the Dutch word for this
encampment being *uitspan*, a place of refreshment and rest, and from this came 'Outspan'.

The grapefruit was introduced into the
United States from the West Indies in about
1890. The large, golden fruits which grew in
clusters, rather like mammoth bunches of
grapes, looked good but no one seemed to
want to eat them. However, one lady tasted
one, liked it, and took several boxes back to
New York, where she gave some to her friends,
who also liked them. Very slowly demand grew
for the grapefruit. At one time it was known as
the Shaddock, after Captain Shaddock, an Englishman who took grapefruit seeds from
Jamaica and planted
them in Barbados.

Probably the first
Britons to taste
lemons were some of
the Crusaders who
spent the winter of
1191–2 in Jaffa,
among the lemon and
orange groves. By the
end of the Tudor
period lemons were
imported in large

numbers from the Mediterranean region, being
particularly valued for their zest – the aromatic
oil obtained from the peel, which was used for
perfumes and flavouring.

Regular exports from Jaffa, then part of
Palestine, began after the end of the Crimean

RIGHT: *Loading the harvest
of South African oranges.*

War. Today many millions of oranges are picked each year in their several hundred orange groves, destined for fruit shops, markets and supermarkets around the world.

The banana originally came from Southern Asia and Indonesia. The fruit was known to both the Ancient Greeks and the Romans, and the Arabs, who traded with India, introduced it to East Africa. Arab slave traders carried the fruit to the west coast of Africa, from where European explorers took the banana plants back with them to the Canary Islands and Madeira. By 1516, bananas were being grown throughout the Caribbean and in Central and South America. In the seventeenth century small ships bound for Europe called at Madeira or the Canary Islands for fresh water and provisions. They carried bananas back to Britain, many deteriorating on the way, but the few that survived were the first seen in England. Steamships, with their shorter journey times, enabled more fruits to survive, although even in the 1870s they were an expensive luxury.

As supplies were irregular, no market was developed for bananas, but barrow boys sold them in the dockland areas of Merseyside and they were also cheaper bought direct from the dockside. By 1888 the Elder Dempster Company, which traded between West Africa and Liverpool and called at the Canary Islands en route, created a separate fruit department, which included bringing bananas into Liverpool.

The Fyffe family had been involved in the tea business since the reign of James I. Edward Wathen Fyffe joined the firm and it became E. W. Fyffe & Son. He married a Miss Brown, but, following childbirth, she became so ill with tuberculosis that they were advised to go to a warmer climate to convalesce. They chose the

However, others, like the pineapple, were already imported, either fresh or in syrup. The pineapple was once referred to simply as a 'pine', due to its shape; although it is not related to pine trees. In the greenhouses and conservatories of many stately homes and large houses, gardeners grew extremely large pineapples for use as table centrepieces. It is thought that eating pineapple after a meal aids digestion.

Canary Islands, and Edward soon noticed the plentiful supply of cheap bananas and looked into the possibility of shipping them to London. He formed an import agency for the growers, and the first sixty bunches arrived in London in September 1888. Soon, small quantities were arriving on a regular basis and were sold to high-class fruiterers. However, in 1897, the growers bought out Fyffe. He retired, but his name had already become synonymous with bananas and this was reinforced when the famous blue 'Fyffes' label was introduced in 1929. By that time they were importing 6 million of the 7 million bunches which came into Britain each year.

In 1894 *Chambers's Journal* mentioned how the 1886 Indian and Colonial Exhibition in London had introduced many previously unknown exotic fruits to the British public – fruits such as mangoes and litchis [sic].

'Reine Claude' was the name given to a plum that was grown in sixteenth-century France, being named after the queen of François I. However, in Britain it became known as the 'Green Gage'. According to a memorandum by Peter Collinson in *Hortus Collinsonianus* in 1843, the plum was brought from France to England by Sir William Gage of Hengrave Hall, near Bury St Edmunds, in about 1725 – hence its name.

The Conference pear was raised by Mr Rivers, a famous nurseryman and fruit grower of Sawbridgeworth, in Hertfordshire. Rivers' nursery was established as early as 1725, and only closed down in 1987. The pear was submitted to the committee of the National Pear Conference in 1885 and thus gets its name; it was the only new seedling to be given a certificate there. It is, of course, renowned for being large and juicy with a delicious rich, buttery flavour and has stood the test of time. The Williams pear is much older, probably having been raised before 1770 by a Mr Wheeler, a schoolmaster of Aldermaston, in Berkshire. He sold his pear to a Mr Williams, who had a nursery at Turnham Green in Middlesex, hence the name. Enoch Bartlett of Dorchester, near Boston, introduced the pear to the United States, where it became best known as the Bartlett pear – a name we also find on tins of pears.

At Easthorpe, in Southwell, Nottinghamshire, stands a cottage which, in 1846, was purchased by one Matthew Bramley, keeper of the nearby White Lion Inn. The cottage had a particularly fine apple tree and, ten years later, this was brought to the notice of Henry Merryweather, the son of a local nurseryman. Messrs Merryweather propagated, exhibited and distributed

plants of it and called it Bramley's Seedling. It is thanks to Celia Steven, a direct descendant of Henry Merryweather, that we can still buy Bramley's Seedling apples, for the European Commission decided it did not fall in line with its policies. However, Celia Steven fought this decision and won the day. In Britain, Bramley is our premier cooking apple.

Another fine apple from the Victorian era is Cox's Orange Pippin. It has been referred to as the queen of dessert apples and some would still say it is *the* dessert apple. Richard Cox was a brewer in Bermondsey, and retired to Lawn Cottage, Colnbrook, in about 1820. He sowed seeds in pots, and from these he achieved Cox's Orange Pippin and Cox's Pomona – both remarkably fine apples. Some local sales of Cox's apple trees took place through Messrs Small, but the apples really came to the notice of the general public when, in about 1850, a Mr Turner of the Royal Nurseries, Slough, promoted them. In 1857 the *Gardener's Chronicle* reported that, at the Horticultural Society's Grand Fruit Exhibition on 24 October 1857, 'In the class of single dishes of dessert kinds [of apples] the first prize was awarded ... for Cox's Orange Pippin, a medium sized, warm looking,

brownish-red variety with a yellow crisp flesh of most exquisite flavour. This was found on this occasion to be greatly superior to the "Ribston", with fine specimens of which ... it was carefully compared.' It was after this that Cox's Orange Pippin rapidly became popular, and has remained so ever since.

In 1838 Maria and Thomas Smith, who were born in Sussex, set sail for a new life in Australia. They set up home in the Ryde district of New South Wales, near Sydney. Their two daughters married two half-brothers who were both local apple growers. By the 1860s Mrs Smith had become a popular figure in the district, and had become affectionately known as Granny Smith. Since her husband was now a semi-invalid she took their produce to the city markets. It is suggested that she was given some fruits of a French Crab variety. Certainly, she was pleased with the cooking qualities of these apples for she later planted their pips. One tree grew and eventually produced fruit, which Granny Smith believed to be an excellent cook-

ing apple. Her sons-in-law began the first plantings, but when large numbers were planted in the colder and drier Bathurst district, the fruit's true potential as a dessert apple was realized. The *Agricultural Gazette* referred to it as Granny Smith's Seedling – and the name stuck.

At a meeting of the Royal Horticultural Society's Fruit and Vegetable Committee in 1897, an Award of Merit was given to 'The Logan Berry', a cross between a raspberry and a blackberry. The loganberry takes its name from Judge James Harvey Logan who, though of Scottish ancestry, was born in the United States. In 1880 he started an experimental fruit garden at his home in Santa Cruz County and the loganberry resulted from planting a row of Red Antwerp raspberries between some wild blackberries. In England, the berry was exhibited by Bunyards Nurseries of Maidstone.

E. A. Bunyard was a well-known nurseryman and horticultural writer of the nineteenth century. Writing about the pea he said: 'even in the thirteenth century the pea was sold in Paris streets ready cooked, and as a soup, and it was not till the time of Louis XIV that it moved from such humble surroundings into royal circles.' Meanwhile in Britain, in the late eighteenth century, Thomas Andrew Knight, a squire, gardener and future President of the Horticultural Society, began experiments in the breeding of peas. The wrinkle-seeded varieties of peas have a higher sugar content than the round-seeded varieties. Today we also have mangetout or sugar peas where we eat pod and all, and the sugar snap peas, which combine a succulent pod with full-sized peas.

The potato is a native plant of South America. It is said that Sir John Hawkins introduced it to Britain in 1563, although generally its introduction is attributed to Sir Francis Drake. On receiving some potatoes from Virginia, the famous botanist Gerard wrote: 'These tubers are nourishing as well as a pleasant dish … whether they be baked in hot ashes, or boiled and eaten with oil, vinegar or pepper …' The potato was widely grown in Europe by the seventeenth century and it became the staple diet of people in Ireland. However, between 1845 and 1849 it succumbed to a blight, causing great famine in the country. The King Edward and Majestic potato were both introduced in the early part of the twentieth century, while potatoes produced in the war years include Home Guard, Arran Victory and Ulster Chieftain. More recent introductions such as Estima, Wilja and Vanessa reflect our stronger links with Europe. Other twentieth-

century varieties have been named after the location of their breeding stations. For example, the Maris Piper and Maris Peer were both bred at the Cambridge Plant Breeding Institute, which is located in Maris Lane, Trumpington, near Cambridge. Similarly the Scottish Plant Breeding Station is based at Pentlandfield, Roslin – hence the Pentland Dell and Roslin Riviera. At Wellesbourne, near Warwick, close to the River Avon, the National Vegetable Research Station has developed a lettuce called Avondefiance, a beetroot called Avon Early, and a parsnip called Avonresister.

The Brussels sprout takes its name from the large acreages of the plant grown around Brussels. The swede was brought to Scotland from Sweden during the eighteenth century, and the Savoy cabbage takes its name from the region of Savoy on the French-Italian border. Similarly, the Cos lettuce is thought to have originated on the Greek island of Cos.

The word 'cauliflower' comes from the old English word 'coleflower', meaning cabbage flower. In the eighteenth century farmers started to grow cauliflowers on a large scale, but in those days they were only a food of the rich. Writer Mark Twain once described it as, 'nothing but a cabbage with a college education'. Today many are grown in Cyprus and imported to Britain.

Carrots are unusual among vegetables in that they have a sweet taste. When honey or sugar were scarce, people turned to the carrot as an alternative sweetener, and of course we now enjoy carrot cake. Carrots did not become a popular vegetable until Elizabethan times. They were once felt to 'excite the passions' and were therefore served to people before romantic occasions. It is likely the vegetable was introduced in the Roman period, but there is some doubt over whether it was the root or its leaf that was eaten.

Parsnips and turnips have both been regarded as foods of the poor and as 'fasting vegetables'.

The beetroot was not widely eaten in Britain until the seventeenth century, although the Romans are known to have eaten it. In 1587 the herbalist Gerard wrote that he had been given a Great Red Beet by 'Master Lete, a merchant of London' who was said to have obtained it from the Mediterranean region.

Rhubarb came to Britain in the sixteenth century from Siberia, but it wasn't until the eighteenth century that its culinary uses were realized. Today, while most gardeners pick their rhubarb 'green' to use in the kitchen, many more housewives look forward to the first pink 'forced' rhubarb of the season. The first recorded forcing took place in Chelsea in 1817, but it wasn't until sixty years later that commercial forcing of the crop took place – in what has become the 'Rhubarb triangle' between Wakefield and Leeds. All Britain's rhubarb is grown in this small area.

Rhubarb roots are placed tightly together in the dark, warm forcing sheds and then watered to clean them of any grit which might scratch the succulent young growths. To prevent the leaves turning from yellow to green, all the picking is done by candlelight; the shoots are then graded before being carefully packed into lined boxes.

Rhubarb is regarded as having health remedy properties due to its acid content, but is also valuable eaten stewed, used in crumbles or as a jam.

Tomatoes originate from Ecuador and Peru, but were first cultivated in Mexico and Central America, before being introduced to Europe in the sixteenth century. The tomato was often known as the 'Love Apple' in early writings, a fruit capable of arousing dangerous passions. In Italy it was known as *pomo d'oro*, meaning golden apple, and also *pomo dei mori*, meaning apple of the moors. However, the French took the latter to be *pomme d'amour*, and the British carried this mistake into our language.

Over the centuries people in Britain have relied heavily on their gardens to provide them with fresh fruit and vegetables although, of course, other exotic varieties have come from around the world. When overseas supplies were cut off during the Second World War many householders 'Dug for Victory' and turned flower beds into vegetable patches. Today health nutritionists encourage us to eat about five fruits or vegetables each day, but it is hoped we enjoy them without such advice.

Just Desserts
CUSTARD, JELLIES & PUDDINGS

Many people hold with the idea that a good meal is not complete without a fine pudding or dessert. Although in recent years this might be in the form of banoffi pie or tiramisu, many people believe that old-fashioned puddings such as jam roly-poly, spotted dick, bread-and-butter pudding or treacle sponge with custard are the best.

Fruit puddings have always been a favourite – a good way of using up fruit that is past its best, or too bitter to eat uncooked. Many puddings, such as the much-loved summer pudding or Eve's pudding, were bulked up with sponge, pastry, bread or breadcrumbs to help

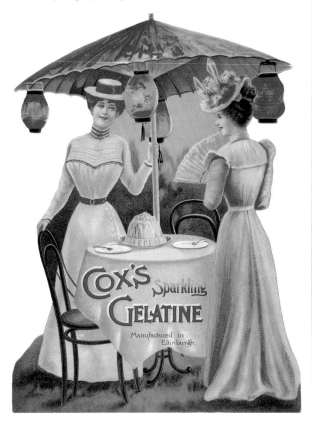

fill hungry stomachs. Apple Charlotte is another such dish – a mixture of apples, breadcrumbs and brown sugar, it is said to be named after Queen Charlotte, the wife of George III.

People have been eating fruit fool since at least the sixteenth century. The name comes from the Latin word *follis*, meaning bellows. In this case it refers to the lightness of the dessert, which is achieved by drawing air into the ingredients while whipping them.

The 1920s and 30s were the heydays of the steamed and baked pudding: fruit, ginger, lemon, toffee, vanilla, treacle, chocolate and jam – each served with a custard sauce. We can thank Alfred Bird for lump-free custard, for in the middle of the nineteenth century he created the first eggless custard. The celebrated 'three birds' trademark was introduced in 1929.

CREAMOLA
Tickles the World's Palate
THE SIGN OF A VERY GOOD PUDDING

CREAMOLA FOOD PRODUCTS Lᵗᵈ GLASGOW

The crêpe suzette is named after a maid in a French Comedy production, who served pancakes to her employers. Crêpes suzettes were first served by the famous French chef, Joseph, at the Restaurant Marivaux in Paris. The pancakes were flavoured with orange and flambéed in liqueur or brandy. Later, Richard D'Oyly Carte bought the restaurant so that he could gain the services of its chef, whom he duly appointed as successor to César Ritz at the Savoy Hotel. Thus crêpes suzettes were introduced to the elite diners of London.

Baked Alaska was actually first baked in China. It is said that it was brought to Europe by the Chinese chef of a Far-Eastern emissary who was visiting Paris and who stayed at the Grand Hotel. It consists of a block of ice cream being placed in a round or oval dish, surrounded by meringue, which acts as an insulator. The French called it *omelette Norvegienne* because of its Arctic appearance; the name 'baked Alaska' came from America. The modern version of the pudding is usually served on a sponge base and can include a selection of fruits both inside and on top of the pudding.

Helen Porter Mitchell was born in Melbourne in 1861 and later trained as an opera singer in Paris with Madame Marchesi. In 1886 it was suggested she should change

BIRD'S
CUSTARD

BIRD'S CUSTARD AND JELLIES

ROWNTREE'S TABLE JELLY DELIGHTS

RUSSIAN CHARLOTTE

CHOCOLATE BLANCMANGE

JELLY MARLBOROUGH

RASPBERRY POMMES

HERE are four attractive dishes made with Rowntree's Table Jellies. The recipes for these, and for many other delightful sweet course dishes, are given in full in *Rowntree's Book of Chocolate & Jelly Dainties.* (Recipes approved by the Good Housekeeping Institute.)*

Whether you are making a simple jelly or an elaborate "sweet" you will find Rowntree's Jellies turn out well—firm, clear and radiant in colour, and above all supremely refreshing in flavour.

The Recipe Book will be sent free for a postcard to Rowntree's, M.1. "Gift" Dept., York. One card will bring the book together with particulars of the delightful gift casket of Chocolates shown overleaf.

10 Varieties   4½ᴰ·
pint packet

Rowntree's TABLE JELLY

her name and thus she became Madame Melba, taking her stage name from her native city. It was said that she sang like a nightingale, and famous composers wrote works especially for her. She sang before Queen Victoria at Windsor and was acclaimed by audiences at Covent Garden. Among her devoted fans was Escoffier, a famous French chef. On one occasion he decided to come up with a dessert in

Brown & Polson's
STANDARD FLAVOUR
CUSTARD POWDER

Nellie's honour. He took a cup and added vanilla ice cream, followed by a peach that had been poached in vanilla syrup. He then covered the contents with crushed raspberries. In her memoirs, Dame Nellie Melba described that special first occasion when she ate the pudding:

> I was lunching alone in a little room at the Savoy
> Hotel in London, on one glorious morning in
> Spring. I was served a most excellent luncheon.
> Towards the end of it arrived a little silver dish,
> which was uncovered before me with a message
> that M Escoffier had prepared it specially for me.
> And much as Eve tasted the first apple, I tasted the
> first Peach Melba in the world. 'It's delicious' I said.
> 'Ask M Escoffier what it is called.' Word came back
> that it had no name, but that M Escoffier would be
> honoured if he might call it Peach Melba. I said he
> might with the greatest pleasure, and thought no
> more of it. But very soon afterwards, Peach Melba
> became the rage of London.

Another lady to be honoured with her own dessert was the Russian ballerina Anna Pavlova. The pavlova, a meringue filled with tropical fruit and topped with whipped cream, was created in the late 1920s after her visit to Australia and New Zealand. Bert Sachse, a chef at Perth's Esplanade Hotel, adapted the recipe from a pre-existing meringue cake, to create a dessert that was as light and airy as the ballerina herself.

Our modern blancmange, which is a mixture of cornflour, flavouring, colouring, sugar and milk and set in a mould, bears little resemblance to those of Victorian times. A recipe from the 1870s tells us to:

> Dissolve in a saucepan, over a very gentle fire, two
> ounces of the best isinglass [a type of gelatin] in
> two pints of new milk. Add the rind of a lemon and
> a pint of cream; boil a quarter of an hour and take
> out the peel. Sweeten, and flavour either with
> cinnamon, rose or orange-flower water, or vanilla.
> While cooling, stir in a little white wine and brandy,
> and pour your blanc-mange in moulds to stiffen.

Jellies today come in easy to use blocks. This was not so in Victorian times when they were made with gelatine, a substance derived from the bones and tissues of animals that had undergone prolonged boiling. It was available in sheets or crystals. To the gelatine, which had to be soaked for a couple of hours, water and fruit was added. If the resultant jelly was a little 'cloudy' it could be made clear by adding whisked white of egg and eggshell to the liquid, before it was then strained through a bag made of coarse woollen cloth or felt. 'Marbled jellies' were quite popular, where the jelly was created in an assortment of different colours.

Today we are more likely to open a tin of creamed rice pudding than to bake a milk pudding in the oven. In *Mrs Beeton's Book of Household Management*, cooks are told to pick [over] and wash the rice, place it in a greased pie-dish, add the sugar, milk and a small pinch of salt, before sprinkling the surface lightly with nutmeg. The dish and its contents are then placed in a 'slow' oven for about two hours. Quite often sultanas would be added to the mixture, and a 'nob' of butter might be placed on the top of the pudding to form a golden brown skin while in the oven.

Invariably if we think of today's tinned milk puddings our mind goes to the Ambrosia brand. Alfred Morris started his venture at Lifton in Devon in 1917. His aim was to produce full-cream dried milk to help the war effort and it was sold through welfare centres as a food for infants. In 1933 Ambrosia was the first to introduce tinned Devon Cream, and in 1937 was also the first to market rice pudding in a can.

We must not forget our most festive of puddings, the Christmas pudding. In medieval times Christmas porridge was made with beef and veal, and was stewed with prunes, currants,

raisins, spices and wine. Over the centuries the meat has been removed and gradually the recipe moved towards our modern-day pudding. The Sunday before Advent in the Church Calendar has the Collect which begins: 'Stir up, O Lord, the wills of your faithful people, that they, bringing forth the fruit of good works, may by you be richly rewarded.' It therefore became known as 'Stir Up Sunday', a reminder to get on with the pudding making. Each member of the family took part, and silver three-penny bits or six-penny pieces were hidden in the pudding mix, ready for some lucky person to find in their serving on Christmas Day.

Of course there are hundreds of puddings, and today's chefs are as eager to come up with new creations as those of centuries past. Sadly old-fashioned puddings seem to be out of favour. I look forward to the day when people's discontentment is put down to pudding deprivation'!

Fair Game
MEAT & POULTRY

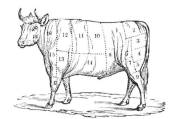

Historically, meat and poultry were something of a luxury, and for many people were only an occasional part of their daily diet. For the gentry, however, meat dishes were in more regular supply – the spoils of a day's hunting or simply culled from domestic animals kept by their tenants.

People's meat-eating habits have changed rather dramatically in recent years. Foreign meat dishes such as curries have become increasingly popular, and even cooking the weekend roast at home is in decline as more people go out and eat at carveries on Sunday. Publicity about the ills of too much red meat has also meant that we are eating more fish and chicken, while the controversy surrounding commercial production of our foodstuffs has led to an upturn in sales of organic meat.

Such concerns are by no means new, however. In 1874 consignments of beef, mutton and poultry were imported into Britain from Canada. Later that year live cattle also followed along the same route to Liverpool docks. There was much concern in England lest the animals should bring in any contagious diseases, and the United States was soon scheduled as an infected area. In 1892 a single case of disease was discovered in Canada, and this was considered sufficient to bring about similar restrictions on Canadian cattle.

For those of us who do still enjoy beef, one of the more favoured cuts is the sirloin. Legend has it that one of our kings – the story is attributed to Henry VIII, James I and Charles II – drew his sword and 'knighted' a choice piece of beef, dubbing it 'Sir Loin'. Indeed, the proprietors of Houghton Tower in Lancashire, which is situated midway between Blackburn and Preston, claim that James I actually knighted the loin of beef there in 1617. There is little

LEFT: *Roast rib of beef.*

likelihood that this is anything more than a legend, for 'sirloin' derives from the Old French word *surlonge*, from *sur* and *longe*, meaning 'above the loin'. Over the years the spelling gradually changed to sirloin. Some people may be lucky enough to have feasted on a baron of beef, which is two sirloins left uncut. Again, rather tongue in cheek, it is said that a double sirloin is of higher rank, and therefore becomes a 'baron' rather than an ordinary knight or a sir.

In his book *Food*, Andre Simon gives details of the meals eaten by the Lords of the Star Chamber in 1520, and these include, 'Beef, a sirloin and a double rump'.

Beef Wellington is still a traditional favourite, being made by wrapping a fillet of beef, covered with a mixture of liver pâté, mushrooms and even brandy, in a puff-pastry casing. Supposedly it looks like a well-polished leather boot, and is said to commemorate Arthur Wellesley, third son of the Earl of Mornington, who was born in 1769 and became the first Duke of Wellington. A frugal eater himself, he is best remembered for his successes in battle, particularly in his victory over Napoleon at Waterloo in 1815. His funeral at St Paul's

1.—Sirloin of Beef.   2.—Boiled Beef.   3.—Roast Aitchbone of Beef.   4.—Roast Ribs of Beef.

Cathedral in 1852 was one of the greatest pieces of ceremonial in British history. It is very unlikely that the dish was named after the Duke in his lifetime, but probably named in his honour after his death.

Yorkshire pudding is always closely associated with roast beef. It was originally cooked beneath the roasting meat, catching the juices as it turned on the spit. In Yorkshire the batter pudding was eaten first as a separate course, which helped to fill the stomach if the joint of meat was a small one.

In Central Asia, during the thirteenth century, Genghis Khan's Tatar horsemen are said to have put pieces of raw steak under their saddles and then ridden on them until they became tender enough to eat without cooking. Today, steak tartar, or tatare, is generally

made with ground fillet steak, which is served with a raw egg and blended with onion, coarse-milled black pepper, salt and tabasco.

Corned beef is an American invention. A 'corn' was literally a small particle, as in corn on the cob or maize, but in this case it referred to the coarse grains of salt that were sprinkled on the cooked beef to preserve it, the sprinkling being called 'corning'. Fray Bentos is the best known trade name associated with corned beef, and was the first to market it commercially. Fray Bentos is actually the name of a port on the River Uruguay in West Uruguay, South America. The area is noted for its meat packing, land and cattle being plentiful, and the river is so wide that sea-going ships are able to sail right up to moor at the town's dock. In the late nineteenth century the Fray Bentos company bought a large estancia there covering 10,000 acres of land, which they later extended by a further 17,000 acres. Eventually they were able to lease 52,000 acres for rearing cattle. They started selling corned beef under the trade name Fray Bentos in 1899 and that same year the company also bought 80,000 acres of grazing land in Argentina. During the First World War 200 million tins of Fray Bentos Corned Beef were supplied to the British armed forces. Today Fray Bentos also make tinned steak and mushroom, chicken and vegetable, and steak and ale pies.

In 1847, Baron Justus von Liebig, a brilliant German chemist, devised a method for extracting and concentrating the goodness of beef. Beef was expensive in Europe at this time, but Liebig wanted to ensure that even poor people could afford his concentrated essence of beef, which was sold in stone jars as a liquid. Liebig promised to reveal his formula to anyone who could discover a way to produce and market the extract more cheaply, while maintaining his high standards. A Belgian engineer called George Giebert heard about this while he was working in Uruguay. He knew that the carcasses of cattle, whose hides had been used for shoe leather, were being left to rot at Fray Bentos, and figured that he could negotiate to buy the meat cheaply. He went to see von Liebig, and in due course came up with an extract that met with the baron's approval. Giebert later bought land and cattle of his own as both were plentiful in Uruguay and could be obtained cheaply. The beef extract sold well and the Liebig's Extract of Meat Company was formed. The extract was used in hospitals and during the Crimean War of 1854–5 Florence Nightingale described it as 'perfectly invaluable' in nursing the sick and wounded. In 1899 the extract's name changed to Oxo and the company's new

chairman, C. E. Gunter, wanted to make the product even more accessible to the general public. Eventually the company came up with Oxo cubes, which were originally hand wrapped and sold at 1d each. They were an immediate success. Oxo Ltd was registered in September 1914, its chairman being Lord Hawke, the President of the MCC and former captain of the Yorkshire County Cricket Club. Oxo Ltd also sent to the British forces during the First World War, supplying them with 100 million cubes.

Who said **BOVRIL**?

from Vrilya, the name given to 'life force' in Edward Bulwer-Lytton's novel *The Coming Race*. John Johnston said the name came to him 'over a cigar'. The first record of Bovril being sold in Britain is in 1886, when there were free tastings at the Colonial and Continental Exhibition in South Kensington.

Another well-loved beef extract is Bovril. John Lawson Johnston, a Scot by birth, started producing tinned beef in Canada. He also experimented with blending meat extract with caramel, salt and spices, and in 1871 produced a spread which could be put on bread or, when mixed with hot water, could be taken as a drink. It was first known as Johnston's Fluid Beef, and later as Bo Vril – which comes from *bos*, the Latin for ox, and 'vril'

Ox roasting was once a way of celebrating major events such as coronations, royal jubilees, peace after war, or the completion of some major project. The passing of the Manchester Ship Canal Bill in 1885 was one such project and there were celebrations throughout Manchester and the surrounding districts. The largest of these was at Eccles in Lancashire, where a crowd of about 100,000 gathered from neighbouring places, coming in by train, tram and omnibus, as well as on foot. Eccles was decorated with flags and strings of banners, and bands played to add to the sense of occasion. The ox carcass was held over the brick oven by a crane and roasting commenced at about 6.30 a.m. A shaft of iron had been passed through the carcass so that it could be turned, and the roasting was

completed by 2 p.m., at which time the meat was raised above the oven to allow everyone to see it. Several members of the crowd took the beast's teeth as souvenirs, but such was the size of the crowd it was decided to defer giving out the meat until the following evening, when slices could be had from Mr Taylor's butcher's shop.

A similar ox roasting had taken place in Clitheroe on 28 June 1838, to celebrate the Coronation of Queen Victoria, and there the superintendent of each Sunday School was requested to go the marketplace immediately after the procession had finished 'to receive a handsome Piece of Ox BEEF, to take to their respective Schools; after which the remainder will be distributed to the Public'.

It was German immigrants who took the hamburger with them to America. It never contained ham but was originally a Hamburg steak, consisting of chopped beef. The Americans converted it to a minced-beef pattie and ate it in a bread bun. It has since become the biggest selling fast-food item in the world.

Mutton stew and mutton chops were once a great favourite with those that could afford them although today we generally prefer the more tender lamb. A South Yorkshire town is particularly proud of having got the chop – the Barnsley chop. This large chop comprises the first three ribs, after the shoulder, of a sheep, and can weigh from 12 ozs to 1 lb 8 ozs, depending on the size of the animal. The culi-

nary 'secrets' are that the meat should be hung for at least ten days before cooking, and that it should be served accompanied by warm potato crisps and Barnsley-brewed bitter beer. Said to have originated at the King's Head Hotel in the distant past, when farmers met there at lunchtime, Barnsley chop was on the luncheon menu when the then Prince of Wales opened the Town Hall in 1933.

With the coming of reliable methods of refrigeration towards the end of the nineteenth century, it became possible to preserve fresh meat for long periods, rather than salting or otherwise curing it. Due to the high price of home-reared meat, refrigerated meat was imported into Britain from abroad. By 1893 it was felt that it was hard even for experts to distinguish cheaper New Zealand mutton from the finest British mutton. To avoid its being passed off as British meat, therefore, it was agreed that carcasses should be branded,

MAKES COOKING SO EASY

The Housewife looks to NEW ZEALAND
confident in the knowledge that while
production increases, the traditional high quality
of New Zealand Lamb is being rigidly maintained.

NEW ZEALAND
LAMB
The Best in the World

other end filled with apple or jam – a two-course meal. It was a meal that a worker might take down a tin mine or out into the harvest fields; one that could be eaten either hot or cold. The pasty originally had two pastry handles at each end, thus it could be held more easily, and this also prevented the food from being soiled by dirty hands. Once the pasty had been eaten, the handles were thrown away. It is said that miners' pasties would be marked with their initials, so that if there were any leftovers these could be identified later on. It was also said that if a pasty were to be dropped from the pit top to the bottom, it would land intact. The Cornish tourist board has something to say on the subject of today's

BELOW: *A side of pork showing cuts of bacon and ham.*

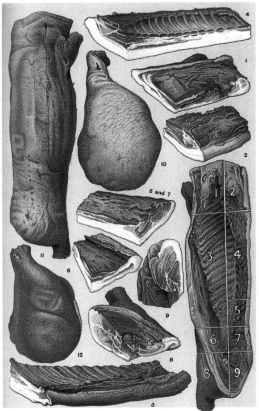

using a platinum wire electrically brought to a white heat, as this did not damage the meat. At this time Australia had 85 million sheep, and 8 million cattle, and was looking to develop a considerable trade in tinned meat, soup, and similar products. It appears that the meat was boiled and then tinned whilst still hot, the cans being soldered up without delay – both the tin and the solder were exported from Britain. The liquor formed during the boiling of the meat was used to make the soup, the fat was turned into butterine, and whatever remained was boiled down to tallow. The larger bones were exported, together with the horns, hoofs, and tail hair; the rest of the bones were ground to dust for fertilizer; only the blood appears to have been discarded.

The Cornish pasty, was often made with mutton, although originally the filling was a fish one. It was a much bigger item of food than it is today, having one end of the pasty filled with meat, potato, onion and seasoning, and the

pasty: 'A home-baked Cornish pasty is never, ever eaten with a knife and fork, although a plate is admissible; is never, ever eaten with vegetables (or, worse still, chips or brown sauce); and never, ever contains diced ingredients – always sliced.' The Cornishman, it is said, can recognize the genuine article at fifty paces with his nose and the Cornishwoman with one glance at the crimping – the pasty should have a rope-like crimping along its side.

In medieval times, December was the month for killing pigs, whose salted or smoked meat was the best that could be had during the long winter months and whose blood and offal could be turned into sausages and stored.

Most of us have heard of Shrove Tuesday, but few people are aware that the previous day is known as Collop or Shrove Monday – a collop being a small piece of meat, which was traditionally eaten with eggs on this day. A copy, prior to 1870, of the *Gentleman's Magazine* states that 'most places in England have eggs and collops [pieces of bacon] on Shrove Monday'.

Bacon has been a popular meat for many years, as we know from the Dunmow Flitch of Bacon. This curious ceremony, nowadays held every leap year, had its birth in the Priory of Great Dunmow in Essex, in 1104, to show that the celibate monks still held the honourable state of matrimony in high regard. The idea was that if a couple could come forward after twelve months of marriage and swear an oath that they had never had a quarrel, had never regretted their marriage, and if again open to an engagement would marry exactly as they had done before, they would be rewarded with a flitch of bacon – a flitch being the side of the pig. The oath had to be made before the prior, the convent and the whole town, humbly kneeling in the churchyard upon two hard, pointed stones. In the fifteenth century there were three successful applications, but over the years the tradition lapsed. However, in 1885 it was revived and it is now a joyful celebration, in which couples have to satisfy a mock

court of judge and jury that they have lived in harmony for a year and a day.

Sausages are well loved – whether as part of the breakfast 'fry-up', bangers and mash or toad-in-the-hole. The origins of the sausage go back a long way. They are mentioned in Homer's *Odyssey*, and in other Greek writings dating back to 900 BC. The sausage was also the subject of a play by Epicharmus, a Greek dramatist, in 500 BC. The Romans were rather fond of their sausages, fresh, dried or smoked, and they called them *botuli*. Sausages had started being divided into links by the time of Charles I and the first skinless sausages became possible when the mixture of meat, herbs and spices was stiffened with eggs and a little wine. A book by Elizabeth Hammond, *Domestic Cookery*, published in about 1830, suggests that a sausage should be fried until it is nicely brown 'or it may be stuffed in well-cleaned hogs' guts, in which case you must add to the meat a fourth part of bread crumbs soaked in water'. She also reminded cooks to prick sausages with a fork before cooking them, in order to prevent them from bursting! Queen Victoria gave out special instructions that sausages for the Royal household should contain meat that was chopped, not minced (so as not to squeeze the juices out), and that the sausage skins were to be filled by hand, pressing down the mixture (which included

beaten egg) through a funnel with the thumbs. Regions throughout the world have their own types of sausages, and individual butchers have their own recipes. The traditional Cumberland sausage, for example, is generally sold as a single, curled sausage and has a chunky, meatier texture than other sausages, whereas the Lincolnshire sausage is of a more open texture than others. Today there is a large range of speciality sausages from spicy chicken, lamb and mint, to salmon. One butcher, Cowmans in Clitheroe, for example, claims no fewer than sixty different flavours, including pork and orange, venison, wild boar and rosemary lamb.

No doubt older readers will remember as children seeing rail trucks distinctively marked with the words 'Palethorpes Sausages', or may remember having a model one in amongst a Hornby train set. A famous name in sausages, along with Wall's and Bowyer's, Palethorpes was established in Gooch Street in Birmingham in 1852. The importing of American bacon had devastated the English bacon trade, but Henry Palethorpe set out on a new

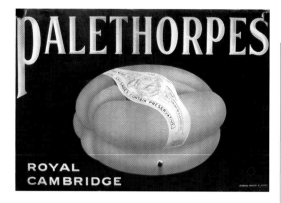

line: 'Palethorpes' Royal Cambridge Sausage'. As the business grew a move was made to the New Model Factory at Dudley Port (later to become Tipton); it took three years to build, and its roofing covered one and a half acres. By 1901 the company was making 35 tons of sausages a week, and over 10 tons of pork pies, and was also selling pressed beef, boneless hams, brawn and bacon, and exporting preserved-meat goods to many parts of the world. The company later moved to Market Drayton in Shropshire, and remained in the hands of the Palethorpe family until 1969.

The frankfurter is a type of smoked pork or beef sausage originally to be found on sale in Frankfurt, in Germany. American soldiers during the First World War called it a 'Victory Steak', but back in America the name 'hot dog' was coined. This name was created by T. A. 'Tad' Dorgan, a prominent sports cartoonist of the period. One of the first people to sell the hot dog as we know it today, along with bun, mustard and relish, was Harry Stevens, who had a food-stall concession at the Polo Grounds, then the home of the New York Giants baseball team. In *Quotations of Our Time* by Laurence J. Peter, the following tribute is paid to the hot dog: 'The noblest of all dogs is the Hot Dog; it feeds the hand that bites it!'

Whilst some of us prefer meat, others are poultry lovers. The ancient Romans considered peacocks to be a delicacy, and all 'people of fortune' had it at their table. In medieval times they were served complete with all their plumage. Later the bird was often contained within a pastry 'coffin', with neck erect and tail expanded above the crust. Swans were once also a delicacy, and although they are now the property of the Queen and her permission must be sought before a swan can be killed, they are still said to appear on the table of at least one Oxford college.

During the eighteenth and nineteenth centuries many of the cottage dwellers of Aylesbury kept ducks – indeed, the area bounded by Castle Street, Whitehall Street and Friarage Road (formerly Oxford Road) was known as 'Duck End'. As a result a particular breed developed, which became known as the Aylesbury duck. These pure-white ducks have a distinctive shape, with orange feet and legs and a bill that is flesh coloured. They were considered by many to be the tastiest in the country and a large number were sent by train to London, where their delicate, light-coloured flesh appeared on the plates of the rich and famous. Mrs Beeton wrote of them in 1861: 'The white Aylesbury Duck is, and deservedly, a universal favourite. Its snowy plumage and comfortable comportment make it a credit to the poultry-yard, while its broad and deep breast, and its ample back, convey the assurance that your satisfaction will not cease at its death.' It is doubtful if any of the original strain still exist, as over the years there has been much cross breeding, but Aylesbury duck still appears on the menu of many fine restaurants.

While Aylesbury is famous for its ducks,

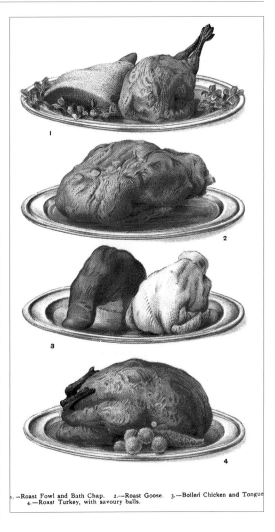

1. —Roast Fowl and Bath Chap.   2. —Roast Goose.   3. —Boiled Chicken and Tongue.
4. —Roast Turkey, with savoury balls.

Nottingham is famous for geese – in particular its Goose Fair. There is an area of the city known as Goose Gate and it was near to here that the annual fair would be held at the end of September, when the labourers also came to the Hiring Fair in search of work. At this time of the year the birds would be plump and good to eat. Norfolk geese used to be driven in flocks to London, taking a couple of weeks. The birds often had special shoes fitted to protect their feet.

The Bible tells us that when the Children of Israel complained of a lack of food as they crossed the desert, God provided them with quails. Today these small game birds, and their

135

eggs, are regarded as being of higher class than other poultry. Chicken is the most common bird to grace our tables, although these days it appears in many guises such as chicken kiev, chicken Maryland or chicken in a basket. Chicken in the rough was devised by an American caterer, Beverley Osborne, in 1937 and was one of the earliest franchise foods. Coronation chicken, a cold chicken dish flavoured with curry powder, was created to be eaten on 2nd June 1953, the day of the Coronation of Queen Elizabeth II, so that those wishing to watch the ceremony on television could do so without having to cook a meal. A more recent chicken dish is chicken tikka masala, which is said to have originated in a London restaurant in the 1970s. The story goes that a customer complained that his chicken tikka was too dry, and so the chef added tomatoes and sauces, thereby creating this anglicized version of the Indian dish.

The turkey was originally native to Central America and was introduced to Europe by Spanish invaders. The Spanish also introduced the bird to North America where it ran wild and became a popular source of food with new settlers – particularly at Thanksgiving. Its name is a misnomer – Europeans mistakenly thought that the bird was a guinea fowl, which were brought from Africa through Turkish territory, and called it a turkey cock.

Some meat dishes have not found their way into regular use, in the case of the Denby Dale pie not least because of its size! The first such pie from this Yorkshire Pennine village, which lies midway between Huddersfield and Barns-ley, was made in 1788 to celebrate George III's recovery from mental illness. In June 1815 the Denby bakers baked a 'Victory Pie' in honour of Wellington's victory at the Battle of Waterloo; it contained two whole sheep and twenty fowl. When the Corn Laws were repealed in 1846 the Denby Dale pie produced for this occasion was of gigantic proportions, being baked in a circular dish that was 7 feet in diameter and almost 2 feet deep – it consisted of seven hares, fourteen rabbits, four pheasants, four partridges, four grouse, two ducks, two geese, two turkeys, two guinea fowl, four hens, six pigeon, sixty-three small birds, five whole sheep, a calf and a hundred pounds of beef! We are told the pie was edible; however, when the supporting platform collapsed the pie broke into pieces and was devoured by the 15,000 crowd, who scrambled to get a taste. The next pie was created to celebrate the Golden Jubilee of Queen Victoria in 1887, but although made by a firm of professional bakers from Halifax, the pie, which was 8 feet 3 inches in diameter, was found to have gone bad during cooking and had to be buried in quick-lime in a nearby wood. To mark its demise the people of Denby Dale produced black-bordered 'funeral cards' and, perhaps to save their pride, the ladies of the village produced their own 'Resurrection Pie' within the same week. This was a complete success. Further pies have been made down the years, including one to celebrate the 200th anniversary of the first Denby Dale pie.

Other pies were of a more practical nature and are still popular, particularly for picnics and buffets. Raised pies were made as a way of letting people hold cooked meat, rather than using a knife and fork, and therefore were an ideal lunch for labourers or people on the move. Pork pies, veal and ham, and game pies are all still popular favourites. Melton Mowbray in Leicestershire has been associated with pork-pie manufacturing for over 150 years, and pork pies are still made there today in the traditional manner. The town has similarly had a long connection with cheese – whey, a by-product of the cheese-making process, being good food for pigs. The first shop to bake and sell pork pies in the town was opened by Edward Adcock in 1831, and was in Leicester Street, next to the Fox Inn yard. Others quickly followed, among them one in Nottingham Street in 1851, owned by John Dickinson who was later joined by Joseph Morris. Today Dickinson & Morris at Ye Olde Pork Pie Shoppe is

the oldest surviving pork-pie bakery in the town. Melton Mowbray pork pies, unlike any others, are baked without the use of a mould or hoop. The resultant pie has bowed sides, unlike those produced in moulds which have vertical sides.

Our story would not be complete without mention of Spam. A form of tinned pork luncheon meat, Spam was introduced to the world by G. Hormel & Co. of Austin, Minnesota in the 1930s. The company ran a competition in 1937 to name its new product, and it is said that Spam is an acronym for **S**piced **P**ork **A**nd

There is no " SPAM " in the shops now. " SPAM " will be available as soon as possible.

"SPAM" is a registered Trade Mark, and can be used only in respect of the product of Geo. A. Hormel & Co., Austin, Minnesota, U.S.A.

Ham. This luncheon-meat product, consisting of chopped ham and pork, was introduced to Britain by members of the US forces stationed here during the Second World War, and because of the rationing of fresh meat it became a prominent part of people's diets. It was said to stay fresh in the tin for up to seven years. It was made for sixty years, but the last British factory to produce it, in Liverpool, closed in 1997; however, it continues to be made in Denmark.

During this century there has been an increase in the number of people who are vegetarians, but meat and poultry are still a major part of the diet of many folk, and are likely to remain so.

Making It Last
SALTING, CANNING & FREEZING

Over the centuries men and women have discovered many ways in which food can be preserved so that it can be available out of its natural season. It was preserved for times when there was less food around, or to enable those involved in warfare or travel to take it with them on long and perhaps dangerous journeys. Today we tend to use 'preserved food', frozen, tinned, or processed in other ways, as a time saving convenience.

The idea of preserving food in airtight containers was experimented with in the 1790s. Napoleon, looking for a way to feed his vast armies, offered a reward to anyone who

LIBRAIRIE GARNIER FRÈRES
PARIS

could invent a practical way of preserving food, other than with spices. The reward was claimed by Nicholas Appert, a French chef, who suggested using stoppered bottles, heated in boiling water.

For hundreds of years many housewives have bottled fruit and vegetables during the summer months, to then be used during the winter. The containers were topped up with syrup or brine, the brine being made by putting 2–3 ozs of cooking salt into a gallon of water. During the Second World War Kilner jars with glass lids, held airtight with rubber seals and screw-type collars, were commonplace in many pantries. Other types of vacuum lids were also available to fit on 1lb and 2lb jam jars.

In 1860 Louis Pasteur had explained the theory of food preservation, using sterilization by heat. He discovered the principle that food put into a container, sealed to keep out the micro-organisms in the atmosphere, and then heated to kill off those in the can, will remain fresh and uncontaminated until the can is opened.

It is thought that Bryan Donkin, of the firm Donkin, Hall and Gamble, had the idea of using tinplate containers, soldered at all the joints to keep them airtight – tinplate is made of sheet steel coated with tin to prevent rusting. Although the cans were originally made by hand, during the nineteenth century the processes became fully mechanized, machines stamping out the can bodies, conveying them through various processes before ensuring that all the seals were airtight. Once the cans had been filled and sealed they were sterilized by steam cooking, the temperatures and time periods varying according to the type of food in the can – some of the largest early cans could hold up to 45lbs of produce. The cans were then cooled in water, before being labelled.

FOWLER'S
Fruit Vegetable & Game
Bottling Outfits

HOW TO BOTTLE

GEO. FOWLER, LEE & Co., Ltd.,
70-78, Queen's Road, READING.

first choice
FOR SECOND VEGETABLE !

Benedict
PROCESSED
PEAS

*. . . rich in body-building protein—
tempting to the jaded palate
—satisfying and delicious*

PACKED BY UNITED CANNERS LIMITED · I PRINCES STREET · HANOVER SQUARE · LONDON · W.I

Del Monte is one of the world's leading canning companies and can trace its roots back to the Californian gold-rush days of 1849. While many thousands sought their fortune from that elusive metal, many others turned to farming, finding that the land not only produced good corn and cattle but also magnificent fruit. However, such were the quantities of fruit produced that local markets could not dispose of it all. Thus small preserving and packaging companies soon developed.

One such company was the San Jose Packing Company, founded by Dr James Dawson and his son Thomas. James experimented in a shed with the preparation of the fruit, while Thomas, a trained tinsmith, sealed metal containers with a soldering iron. This company, along with 17 others, formed the California Fruit Canners Association in 1899, and adopted the Del Monte label as their premier brand. The name Del Monte was taken from the prestigious Hotel Del Monte in Monterey. In 1916 the Californian Packing Corporation was

formed, with Thomas as their general superintendent – the UK Del Monte product range was established in 1926.

Today fruit is graded, cleaned and peeled, and cut or sliced as necessary at the cannery. To avoid bruising, fruits may travel over a flow of water, but are then carefully placed into the tins – up to 300 tins being filled each minute. The preparation of fruit cocktail is a complex operation often using both previously-canned fruit, and fresh fruits such as grapes, which have come straight from the plantations. Controlled amounts of syrup or fruit juice are added to the fruit before the tins are sealed and steam sterilized. Only cooling and labelling is needed before the can makes its long journey to our table.

In the 1870s there was concern that whilst there were vast acreages of land devoted to rearing meat animals, they were all many thousands of miles away from Britain, in countries

"She's been picked for
Batchelor's
where the best *Peas* go!"

such as Australia, Canada, Uruguay and Argentina. The problem was how this meat could be brought in good condition to British butchers.

Already people were accepting that to transport the live animals was inhumane and uneconomic, and that it must come as preserved meat. Traditional methods of salting were felt to be unacceptable, except in the case of bacon, because any resultant lean meat was often tough and indigestible. Fish merchants often salted fish to preserve it, and this had to be soaked for 24 hours to remove the salt before it could be used.

Scurvy was at that time thought to come from eating salted meat, and many sailors died from the disease. Experiments were carried out to preserve meat – from infusing it with sulphuric acid, to packing it in ice and other low-temperature methods. Meat was also canned or sold as meat extract.

Eggs have not always been readily available throughout the year, and to ensure that households would have eggs throughout the winter some were 'put down' when they were plentiful. Mrs Beeton recommends that the eggs should be covered all over with butter, lard or oil before being placed in a box on a thick

layer of bran, each egg also being surrounded by bran to ensure that they do not touch, and each layer being covered with a similar layer of bran. Some people may remember their grandmother placing eggs in an earthenware bread barrel that contained water glass, sometimes erroneously called isinglass. There was also a

and 'fresh' eggs, six months old, from Russia and the United States. Frozen butter was imported from Australia, Holland and Denmark, while milk, frozen solid, came from Norway.

In the United States and Canada, from about 1935, people had access to frozen-food locker plants; families could rent a locker which held about 6 cubic feet of frozen food. At the centre meat would be cut up into joints and steaks, and fruit or vegetables would be packed in special wax-proof paper packets before the item was frozen. It would then be quick frozen before being locked away in the individual locker, ready for the housewife to get out some months later, thereby providing fruit and vegetables out of the normal season.

The frozen locker idea probably did not come to Britain, and it was not until after the Second World War that frozen foods really started to become popular here, although some refrigerators had been available before this. In 1951 Electrolux were advertising that their refrigerators could be run by electricity, gas or oil.

During the 1960s–1980s home freezing was very popular, with many people freezing their own fruit and vegetables, as well as buying large quantities of meat to freeze. It was com-

preparation called Oteg, a thin preparatory liquid in which eggs were dipped and then stored in baskets for up to about ten months.

Chambers's Journal published details of research carried out in Germany where several different methods of preservation were tried. However, the most successful was a French one, where 4ozs of beeswax were heated with 8ozs of olive oil and the eggs were then dipped in the warm solution, wiped, and stored in charcoal in a cool situation. Of course hard-boiled eggs have been pickled in vinegar for many years.

In the 1880s experiments had been ongoing with refrigeration, and later with freezing food. At first frozen meat was looked at with suspicion, but by the beginning of the twentieth century one third of all meat eaten in Britain was imported by this method. Frozen fish such as Canadian salmon, often weighing from 15lbs to 45lbs each, were also being imported. At the turn of the century thousands of turkeys were imported from Canada for the Christmas trade, fowl from Russia, geese from France and Italy

mon to see families visiting 'pick-your-own' farms, and then taking home produce to freeze in foil or Tupperware-type containers, in the large chest freezers which were often kept at the back of the garage.

Possibly the best known name in frozen foods is Birds Eye. There never was a Captain Birdseye, but there was a Clarence Birdseye! He was a fur trapper and biologist who went to Labrador during the period 1912–15. On his expeditions he noticed that the local people froze fish and caribou meat, and that even after several months it still tasted as good as fresh food. Gradually he realized that it was the

speed of freezing which was important; rapid freezing produced small ice crystals, whereas slow freezing produced large crystals which badly affected the food.

In his laboratory Birdseye tried to recreate the effects of nature, but it wasn't until the early 1920s that he was able to produce a commercially viable freezing system. In 1924, at Gloucester, Massachusetts, he formed the General Seafood Corporation, but as progress was so slow he sold the rights to the Postum Company, which later became General Foods. Sales of frozen foods were slow to take off, but today the frozen-food market is a multi-million-pound business, and Birds Eye is the largest frozen food company in Britain.

Today most people prefer to buy ready-prepared foods from the supermarket rather than bottling, canning or freezing foodstuffs themselves. We live in an 'instant' society and with many of us having full-time employment we have little time to spare to prepare and preserve produce.

Final Word

What a rich food heritage is ours today! Our diet is made up of ingredients from almost every part of the world, which have been brought together by skilled chefs, food technicians and not least by those in individual homes who enjoy creating attractive and delicious dishes.

The story of food is one of kings and rulers, of wealthy merchants and of ordinary people, both at home and in far-off lands. I hope readers have enjoyed the stories, anecdotes, advertisements and other pictures in *How It All Began in the Pantry*. Such material is all part of our social history and is far too valuable to be cast aside when people die, or hidden away in books placed on a shelf to gather dust and perhaps never to be read again.

Over the years our expectations have changed. No longer do many households have a 'baking day', as our grandmothers did. However, perhaps occasionally we ought to get out their old recipe books and rediscover some appetizing treat of our childhood days – that Simnel cake, the jam-sponge pudding with custard or the home-made bread. Go on, spoil yourself!

Picture Credits

The majority of pictures for this book were provided by myself and my wife, Judith. However, we should like to credit the following for the use of their illustrated material: Sally Lunn's Refreshment House & Museum, Bath: p.6; The Chelsea Bun House, The Royal Borough of Kensington & Chelsea Libraries and Arts Service: p.10; Lancashire Eccles Cake Ltd: p. 10; Bakewell pudding, Derbyshire Libraries: p.11; Mr Kipling logo, compliments of Manor Bakeries: p 13; Lyons' Corner House, Lyons Cakes: p13; Goodfellow's Dundee Cake, Goodfellow & Steven: p14; Newens' Maids of Honour Shop, Richmond: p16; The Sea Fish Industry Authority: pp. 26, 27, 32, 33, 34; Douglas West Collection, © Whitstable Musem & Gallery: pp.31 (*top right*), 32 (*top left*); Harry Ramsden's: p. 37 (*top and below*); The National Federation of Fish Friers Ltd: p. 37 (*centre*); Quiggin's, Kendal: p. 41 (*below left*); Everton Toffee Shop, Liverpool Record Office, Liverpool Libraries and Information Services: p.42 (*below left*); Blackpool rock, Peter Bullock and Dennis Broadbent: p.42 (*below right*); Warburtons Limited: pp. 55 (*below right*), 60 (*both*); Rank Hovis McDougall Ltd: p.56 (*top right*); The Stuart-Liff Collection: p.61 (*top left*); Wilkin & Sons Ltd: pp.63 (*below right*), 66 (*below left*); Chivers Hartley Ltd: pp. 64 (*both*), 65 (*below left and right*), 66 (top right), 69 (*below left*) ; Robertson's Golly: p.67; Duerr's: p.67 (*below*); McCormick Europe: p.72 (top); Unilever: pp. 75 (*top left*), 77 (*below left*), 79 (*top left and right*), 80 (*below left*), 91 (*top left and below left*), 92 (*below right*), 106 (*top left*), 108 (*top right*), 129 (*below left*), 130 (*below right*), front cover (Wall's) and back cover (O.K. Sauce); J.N. Nichols (Vimto) PLC: pp.83 (*top left*), 85 (*top right*); Baxters: p.86 (*top right*); National Dairy Council: pp. 96, 97 (*both*), 101 (*top right*); Ian Dewhirst, MBE: p.105 (*below right*); Eden Vale: p.106 (*below right*); Meat and Livestock Commission: p. 126 (*below*); Fray Bentos, Campbell Grocery Products: p. 128 (below left); Wall's Sausages, Kerry Foods: p. 134 (*top right*); NFU Mutual and Ken Griffiths: back cover (kippers).

We would also like to thank the following picture libraries: **The Advertising Archives**: pp.63 (*left*), 87 (*top right*), 90 (*top right*), 102 (*top left*), 103 (*top left*), 104 (*below*), 138 (*top*), 140 (*below*); British Museum, London, UK/**Bridgeman Art Library**: p.70 (*below*), signed A.S; **Hulton Getty**: p.89 (*top*); **Mary Evans Picture Library**: pp. 16 (*top right*), 18 (*below left*), 19 (*top right*), 21 (*below left*), 27 (below), 28 (*top*), 29 (*top*), 30 (*below left*), 31 (*below right*), 35 (*top left and right*), 55 (*top left*), 57 (*below right*), 58 (*below left*), 71 (*below left*), 75 (*top right*), 87 (*below*), 98 (*top*), 122 (*below*), 132 (*top*), 138 (*below*), 139 (*below left and right*).

We also acknowledge use of illustrations from Dover Publications Inc., New York.